NOBODY CARES
How to Be Independent

DARA LY

Copyright © 2023, Dara Ly. All rights reserved.

This book is licensed for your personal enjoyment only. It may not be resold or given away to other people without prior agreement from the author. If you would like to share this book with another person, please purchase an additional copy for each recipient. If you're reading this book and did not purchase it, or it was not purchased for your use only, please kindly purchase your own copy. Thank you for respecting the work of the author.

Table of Contents

PART 1 | FIND THE PROBLEMS 1
Chapter 1 | The Trends | Social Media.................................. 2
Chapter 2 | The World | Forget the World for a While..... 5
Your Priority 7
Chapter 3 | The Issues | The Issue with Mindset 9
The Issue with a Relationship... 10
The Issue with Interest 11
The Issue with Learning 12
Chapter 4 | The People | Being Nice 13
Friendship 14
Dramatic People 16
Toxic People... 17
Chapter 5 | The Relationship | A Failed Relationship..... 18
You Are on Your Own 20
Control Your Chat 21
Chapter 6 | The Expectation | Do Not Expect 22
Limiting & Upgrading 26
Chapter 7 | The Comparison | When I Was Young 27
Comparison 28
Make Your Own Rules 29
Failures 30
Chapter 8 | The Criticism | If you have never been......... 31
Keep That in Mind 32
Confidence... 33
Chapter 9 | The Fears | Before 30 Years Old 35
After 30 Years Old 37
Chapter 10 | The Reminding | Random Reminders 39
PART 2 | FIND THE SOLUTIONS 43
Chapter 11 | Time | Your Time Is Limited 44

Be Very Selective 47
Stop Delaying 48
Chapter 12 | Work | To Leave or to Stay 49
Motivation for Work 50
Do Not Get Too Comfortable 54
Chapter 13 | Mindset | The World Is Not Always Fair 55
Discipline 56
Balance 57
Be the Winner 58
Chapter 14 | Freewill | Freedom 59
You Are the Boss 61
Chapter 15 | Independence | Planning 63
Big Pictures & Details 64
The World Doesn't Owe You Anything 65
Chapter 16 | Courage | Fear 67
How to Be the Best 69
Chapter 17 | Control | No Need to Rush 71
At Home 72
At Work 73
Stay Silent 75
Chapter 18 | Decisiveness | Goals 77
Balance 78
Patience 79
Progress 80
Interested or Not Interested 81
Chapter 19 | System Upgrade | The Right Way 82
Your Life 83
Information 85
Chapter 20 | Nothing and Nothing | Maturity 87
Two Things You Should Care 88
As a Teenager 89

PART 3 | THE TURNING POINT 90
Chapter 21 | Value | The Valuable Lessons 91
Know Your Limits 94
Believe in Yourself 95
Chapter 22 | Self-Development | If You Fail, You Fail 96
No Excuse 97
Study 98
Reading 99
Chapter 23 | High Achiever | Hard Times 100
Reshape Your Life 101
You Are on Your Own 102
High Achiever 103
Stay Strong 105
Chapter 24 | Change | Reverse 106
Game Changer 108
Your Will 110
Timeline 111
Your Freedom 113
Chapter 25 | Money | Money 114
The Rules 116
Chapter 26 | Time to Choose | Morning Motivation ... 118
Time to Choose 120
Chapter 27 | Time to Create | You Are the Creator 122
Hard Times 123
Hopelessness 124
Keep Moving 125
Ignore Your Pain 126
Chapter 28 | Maturity | Transformation 127
Chapter 29 | Because I Am Weird | My Experience with Digital World 132
Chapter 30 | Nobody Cares | Nobody Cares 135

Suggestion from Machine 137
Because I am too busy! 138

Legal Notice

The author has strived to be as accurate and complete as possible in the creation of this book, notwithstanding the fact that he does not warrant or represent at any time that the contents within are perfectly accurate due to the rapidly changing nature of information transformation.

Although all attempts have been made to verify information provided in this book, the author assumes no responsibility for errors, omissions, or contrary interpretation of the subject matter herein.

Any perceived slights of specific persons, people, or organizations are unintentional.

In practical advice books, like anything else in life, there are no guarantees. Thus, readers are cautioned to rely on their own judgment about their individual circumstances to act accordingly.

This book is not intended for use as a source of professional advice. The readers are advised to seek services of competent professionals in the fields.

Acknowledgments

First of all, I'd like to thank my editor Sovanchanbomey Chith. Once again, with your great patience in editing, this book is made possible.

I also want to thank my illustrator Champey Ouk for another beautiful book cover design.

I want to thank the fans of DARA LY Books for supplying many meaningful stories and ideas. You own a big part of this book.

Last but not least, I'd like to thank *Draft2Digital* for publishing this book. Thank you for your great service.

Dedicated to DARA LY Books Fans!

About the Author

DARA LY is the graduate from the University of Puthisastra (UP), bachelor degree of English Literature. He's the Chairman of DARA LY Books, a small book publishing group serving the readers on the topics, such as education, inspiration, and entertainment.

As a lifelong reader, he has founded **DARA LY Reading Space** to open the study clubs for the young generation of Cambodia. He is determined to keep his clubs free of charge, as always.

Since September 5, 2016, Dara Ly has published 16 books, all are for teenagers in Cambodia. His goal is simple (and he's silly enough to pursue it). He wants to encourage young Cambodian people to read 50 books a year.

Introduction

The book "**Nobody Cares**" reminds the readers what they have forgotten. More importantly, it provides a few ideas for people to think and reflect. There are three parts which illustrate thirty chapters.

Part 1: Find the Problems! In this part, the readers will find ten different problems that they might face each day.

Part 2: Find the Solutions! It offers ten solutions for the readers.

Part 3: The Turning Point! The readers may find some surprising facts as well as motivational messages in this part.

In short, this book offers a strange concept for you to think and reflect about your life. If you care about it, you should read "**Nobody Cares**" and find out more.

Good luck, **My Reader!**

PART 1
FIND THE PROBLEMS

Chapter 1
The Trends
Social Media

We live in the era of social media, and we are, in so many ways imaginable, encouraged or manipulated into creating contents to get attention from others. Deep down, we know some of those contents are weird, if not crazy, but we are influenced to follow the trends. By the way, correct me if I'm wrong because I have never followed any trends or stuff being fed on social media.

My point is that we create contents because we want people to care. I don't want to say that we want to seek attention from others even if it might sound closer to the truth.

Having said that, I never deny the fact that we all need to learn and absorb information, on daily basis. That's when good content creation has to play the role. Let me put it this way: High-quality content creation!

I could be wrong, though, but my understanding, as a content writer, is simple: You only produce and keep the contents that can help people. Useful contents, if you will!

I get rid of bad contents that I have produced so far, and it's a painful process. I simply get rid of those rubbish contents that I have published so far. The urge to upgrade is unending, and I am driven by it, so I simply follow what has been presented in front of me. In other words, I'm so busy with my life that I do not have time to follow the trends!

NOBODY CARES

A piece of advice, which I will never advise anyone, to you is this: "Don't follow anyone else's advice without checking the fact first." That also includes this one. Okay?

It takes me several months to write and publish a book, but it takes me more than three years of studying and contemplating the needs of the audience before starting to work on that one simple project! I invest too heavily on each project, although, on the surface, it looks effortless. To me, content creation is a serious job, and you ought to keep it that way if you want to make serious incomes and become successful. Many people have tried and failed because they simply overlook this simple fact.

The point is, if something is really important and timelessly necessary for many people, the investment in researching and studying is worthwhile. On top of that, you're not creating rubbish work; you're creating creative work, so you should know better about the differences between rubbish and creative stuff. Been there, done that. Still trying to get rid of the rubbish part, if you want to know the truth.

My secret to making a good content that people care is to simply treat it as if nobody would care about it. It'll open up your creative part and total freedom to create what you are creating, without the need to worry about self-censorship.

Having said that, the editing part is the opposite point of view, meaning that you are going to treat your work differently from when you are creating it. Simply put, creating process is only the beginning, but changing (editing) it is the continuity of the work until it gets finished properly and beautifully.

The secret of my work is one word: "Nobody cares!" Okay, those are two words, but you get the point, right? If you want to become a successful artist, go for it because nobody cares. If you want to become the best scientist in the world, go for it because nobody cares. If you want to be a good student, focus on your study; do not focus on your classmate. I know, he's cute, but focus on your study now. Okay?

The point is, nobody cares about your life more than you do, and nobody has the rights to change that fact without your authorization. You hold the key to your life, so stop caring about what other people may think or say about you.

What I have learned is this: **Nobody cares about what you do as long as you do not break the laws**. You just have to live your own life by yourself and be good to others the way you want them to treat you. That's a fairly acceptable way of living in a society. Don't you agree?

Why would I want to talk to anyone who doesn't want to talk about my life or my work? I don't have time for that. I wouldn't want to waste anybody's time either. People are busy with many things, and they have no time for other things because they do not care! That's okay because I wouldn't care either.

Get yourself together and work hard for your future. Be the best you can be. This is your time. This is your victory. You are here to win. Focus on your work and your life! Do not follow the trends!

Just to remind you: Please do not follow this advice either! Only you can choose! Only you know what's best for yourself!

Chapter 2
The World
Forget the World for a While

Many people are convinced that they are right about almost everything, and they want others to believe the same things, the same way. There are a lot of "how to" tips being shared on social media platforms, and there are countless experts nowadays.

Call me an isolated person, or whatever you want, but I don't need to know the stories of some random strangers on social media. For all I care, they can do whatever they like as long as they do not harm or hurt me in any manner. What they like has nothing to do with me, and I don't give a damn, in all fairness. Just to be clear, I have no problem with anyone who wants to spend more time on social media. I don't care because I don't live anyone else's life.

Ignore the rest of the world for a while because you have an important job to do, and that is to finish your project. That's all you need to care right now. Keep your mind in that specific frame until you've done your job.

Forget the world for a while; you have a job to do. Ignore your friend's drama for a while; you have a project to complete. Care no more about the other people's problems; mind your own business from now on.

Work hard in silence and ignore the noises around you. First, it's hard, but you must resist and endure until you can overcome those challenges. One small step at a time!

DARA LY

Everything can distract you, and everyone can be a problem for your work. But don't let any of them stop you from working. You have to be serious about that, or you won't have time for your work or project at all.

There are many things in this world that can ruin your life if you allow them to. But will you? No, you won't and you shouldn't. You must fight for your future. And fight for what you want because nobody will give it to you. You have to earn it. You know that better than anyone else, so stop acting like you deserve it without working hard to attain it.

You may have a good day, or you may have a bad day at work, but you can't use it as an excuse to blame yourself or others for what has happened. You must work hard every single day. If you want to be the best, hard work is the only way you can get there.

You have a good day? Good, get to work!

You have a bad day? Fine, now get back to work!

You have to be strong because nobody cares if you have a bad day. Get yourself together and get back to work. Okay?

Try your best! You'll be surprised at how far you can go and how much you can accomplish if you only pursue it in the level you have never or rarely taken before. You'll feel like you have exhausted everything you have, but that's not true. You still get some more, but it's hidden somewhere. Dig deeper and you'll see it. Keep searching, and you'll find just what you need.

Your Priority

When you know that every action you do will have an impact on your future, however good or bad, you'll be more careful with what you do every day. You'll be more selective in food you eat, for example. You'll be far more cautious about what you read from the Internet. Nonetheless, it's not just what you do that may impact your future; it's what you haven't done that can block greatness from reaching you.

Your brain is flexible and adaptive when it comes to physical work as well as mental work. At one point, it will reach a new shape, but only after intense repetition. To make that shape permanent, it has to go through a repeated circle.

Exercise your brain every single day and never expect anything less than what you have accomplished so far. In other words, don't settle for less than what you can do. Sometimes you don't see it, but the progress has been made, however small it may seem. But it's there, waiting for your recognition.

Get some rest when you're tired. Push yourself again after you're fully recharged. Fix errors when you've made some. Learn from good practices when you've done so. You're the boss, so take control of your work!

Slow down when you're tired, but don't stop. Rest when you're tired, but don't expect anything less than what you can do. Recharge your energy when you're exhausted, but never neglect your responsibilities.

Know your priority and stick to what's important at this point. Don't just prioritize everything when you cannot handle it. Many people have tried and failed miserably because they underestimate the impact of mountainous tasks in a short length of time. Don't fall into the same trap.

Chapter 3

The Issues

The Issue with Mindset

The way to find out whether you have what it takes to become successful is to try it. Most people will try for a few times, and they will quit because they're weak-minded. But don't take my word for it. You can do whatever you want. It has nothing to do with me, by the way. Who am I to tell others what to do?

Most of what you believe to be true doesn't have to be necessarily true if you are clueless most of the time. But through times and experiences, you become more informed and your judgment gets better and more accurate in judging the situations or the people around you.

You could be wrong many times about many things before you could get just one thing right for once. You could experience many errors and many failures before you could succeed in doing something. It's a painful process, and anyone who tells you otherwise is either a fool or a liar. You can't grow up if you don't learn from your experiences.

Most of them are not pretty, but the funny part is that you learn better from ugly teachers. No offense to your high school teachers! But you get the point, right?

Hard times make you strong. Ugly experiences give you wisdom and better judgment. There is more to life than you ever thought because with a new and improved mindset comes new ideas and strategies to improve your life.

The Issue with a Relationship

My time is limited, so I won't be spending any of it with anybody who is a distraction. I know whom I love and accept, although she may have some flaws. Who hasn't? Only God is perfect!

I intend to accept her and learn to live with her just like she does for me. A relationship and/or marriage, to me, is an agreement honored by both sides, under certain rules or conditions. If someone tells you that he or she loves you unconditionally that person is either a liar or a fool.

Nobody will love and accept you unconditionally, unless he or she is lying to you.

Don't take my word for it. Listen to your heart and decide! If you still have it!

The Issue with Interest

Most of the things that you choose are determined by only two factors: **Interested** or **not interested**.

If you're interested in being rich, you'll work hard. If you're not interested in hard work, you may have a difficult life. If you're interested in happiness, you'll find the way to be happy. If you're interested in drama, you'll be consumed by drama. I wish I could say otherwise, but it is what it is.

Most of us think that we are helpless in choosing what we want, but nothing could be further from the truth. What you have comes from what you choose, whether you're interested or not interested.

For me, I'm only interested in a few things: being wealthy, healthy, and happy.

The Issue with Learning

There are many ways to reach your goal, but which way is the best? There are many books that can guide you through, but which author do you prefer? There are countless schools that are providing knowledge and education, but what kind of knowledge or education are you seeking?

How to become independent learner? That's the question I've been trying to answer. In other words, I'm still searching for the answer for that. I don't want to sound like an expert, but personally, I rely on my own judgment and research when it comes to finding a certain type of knowledge.

I wouldn't recommend anyone about anything.

That's just not my way!

Even in this book, all I'm doing is remind people what they have forgotten. Simply put, this book talks about the issues that people think but do not speak out. Those thoughts have been stuck in their mind for so long that they become blurry. Some people could hardly recognize some of these issues, but that's okay because nobody cares!

Chapter 4
The People Being Nice

You should see why people don't take you seriously even though secretly they admit that you are right. The reason is obvious; you are too nice and too easy-going. You forgive people even when they make unforgivable mistakes. Some people even make those mistakes on purpose because they know you will always forgive them and be good to them even if they do bad things to you. They think that you are naïve and too good a person.

It is good to be fair, and bad people who treat you unfairly should not be considered your friends. The truth is, they're not your friends at all. They never were. A good friend would never play another friend for a fool. A good friend should not intend to hurt a friend.

Friendship

I'm a kind person by nature, but after a few bad experiences brought to me by bad and dishonest people, I have come to an understanding that if you are too kind yet too blind to see that some people only want to take advantage of your generosity, then you will be a victim of their deception. At times, it is your friend who disappoints you more than those who are not. You often wonder why he or she can do that. The answer itself is forever a mystery to you, for you can never believe that your friend is the worst kind of human being. You are left with disappointment after he or she has let you down. You are kind enough to give your friend a second chance, but it's a gesture to be unappreciated repeatedly by that person. At one point you are faced with a question: *"Should I cut off my friendship with that person?"*

A friend who doesn't appreciate your time and effort for him is not a good friend, and he should not remain in your friend list.

A friend whom you cannot trust is not a good friend, and he ought to be gone from your life because you cannot afford to have such a bad friend.

A friend who only wants to take advantage of the friendship is not a good friend, and you shouldn't keep him as a friend. You don't have to hate him, but you won't ever like him the same way you did. Your idea about him will never be the same again.

A friend who only brings you trouble shall never be considered a good friend.

NOBODY CARES

A friend who only comes to you when he needs something from you should never be considered a good friend, and you should be careful with him.

If you are fair-minded, you will see the real friends and can distinguish them from fake and bad friends who only wish you harm. You should be very careful about whom you befriend, and you should be selective too.

Dramatic People

People have their own problems, and you have yours, so you don't have to tell the world about every single issue that you have because nobody cares. The same can be said about you; if somebody tries to get you involved in his or her personal drama, you wouldn't care, right?

There comes a time when all you want to do is stay away from some people because you're fed up with their unending drama being thrown at you. They try to get you involved in this pointless drama even though it has nothing to do with you at all.

You just can't stand these people, but you can't tell them that they're full of themselves. You don't want to tell them that they are wasting your time because you are a nice person. As a result, they keep demanding your help. Why? Because, once again, you're a nice person!

Berm: "*Yeah, good for you!*"

If your life is not difficult enough, the drama will make it so, and you will be thrown into the unending drama circle that only ceases when you stop feeding it. It's easier said than done. Drama makes you emotional, and your emotions can draw your attention for as long as you care. Drama is something you want to avoid, but it doesn't go away easily. When you are not careful, it will get to you and make your life miserable, for a very long period of time.

To minimize that, you should avoid anything and anybody that can possibly bring more drama to you. It is more likely to happen for dramatic people. Avoid them as much as possible!

Toxic People

How do you deal with toxic people? How do you handle these people? But how do you define toxic people? I mean, they talk and walk just like everyone else. They're not crazy people who do crazy things. At least, not obviously!

Nevertheless, the toxic people are everywhere, and they want everyone to feel sorry for them because of some unfortunate things that have happened to them. Those are the things that have nothing to do with you at all.

Chapter 5
The Relationship
A Failed Relationship

A failed relationship that has been agreed to break apart is but a memory that should be buried, not remembered! The person who has left should be remembered no longer. A new lifestyle should be encouraged, but it has to be better and more harmonious than the previous one. Otherwise, what's the point?

You have experienced enough pain, and you can judge whether a new relationship will bring the same type of pain or not. It's better to stay single for a while if you are unsure of the next relationship.

By the way, nobody cares if you are single or taken, so you don't have to worry whether your parents will force you to get married or not. They will try, but that's okay because you won't agree. Soon, they'll stop forcing you. And again, nobody cares!

No matter how much you love someone, you should let her go if she is unhappy with the relationship. You might have a different idea about a relationship, so you can never be the person she can and will accept. That is just the fact that you cannot change. Why try? I mean, after a dozen times of failures, why bother to convince her otherwise? She won't care! You have a different way of life, and she has her own. Both of you can never get to the agreeable relationship because of the gap between your ideas and hers is just too big!

NOBODY CARES

You can be sad or even depressed, but nobody cares. Stop trying to draw attention for something that nobody gives a damn about. You wouldn't give a damn if it was not your problem, right? Why should you make others care? You may not agree with that idea right now, and that's okay. When you experience that, you will know it. And you're welcome!

You Are on Your Own

Nobody cares about you or your problems. Stop trying to ask for help from anyone. You are on your own now, and you are going to be alone for a long while. Your life is not the problem, but your mind creates it.

Every time you go through the breakup, a piece of your love is torn apart with it too. Every time you go through it, you lose a part of yourself too. We deal with love problems all the time, and we should not add any more than we have to. If possible, try to avoid as many as you can.

You can't afford to be with a dramatic person and expect to have a normal life. It's not going to work out well. You know that better than anyone else, but you pretend that you can stay in this toxic relationship. One day, it will ruin your life in a big way.

Control Your Chat

People have many things that need to be dealt with, so they do not have time for your drama. You ought to stop spreading it.

Friendly Reminder: *"No matter what, don't fall in love too soon. Not yet."*

You don't have to control your heart. Just control your chat! Stay single, and stay positive!

Sometimes all you need is alone time. It might sound corny, but it is true. You will have a clear mind when you stay alone for a while. Your life is your choice to make, and you ought to choose the right things. Your time is limited, so it's advisable to be selective.

Why can't you just stay single for a while? Why do you need a relationship? You're too young, and you know that! What's the point of getting your heart broken repeatedly? Why don't you just stay single for a while? I mean, maybe it's good to heal a wounded heart before you get involved in an uncertain relationship with a new person. What do you say?

Chapter 6
The Expectation
Do Not Expect

Nobody cares whether you're financially free or struggling in this society. Everyone is busy dealing with his or her own problems, so do not expect much help on the way. It will take forever to come. The better option is to rely on yourself although it is expected to get tough from the beginning.

Nobody cares about your miserable life, so do not expect anything from anyone unless you want to be more disappointed than you already are.

Many people expect a lot from the world even though they know it is pointless to do so, in additional to disappointment that they've got from their blind hope. Do not fall into the same circle.

You have to be strong. You have to be tough. You have to be independent. From now on, you don't need any help from anyone else because only you can help yourself in a way that doesn't make you feel guilty. The point is, when you ask for help from others, you owe them something. When you cannot return the favor, you feel guilty. Guilt is something you can't stand, and you shouldn't add it up to your life if it's not necessary. Maybe it sounds weird, but deep down, you agree with me.

You're born for greatness, and you should remind yourself that. All the obstacles that stand in your way will vanish once your greatness has been realized. You're the only person who

NOBODY CARES

can discover it. To be able to do so, you must embrace yourself and everything else that is made to strengthen and sharpen your mind and heart. Forget the old things that didn't help you grow; they're all but memories!

Forget those who have forgotten you. Forget them, and you shall be free, mentally, and emotionally. You can't afford to get stuck in a bad place with people who see no value in your friendship. Let them go, and you will have a better life. You know that, and they know that too.

You are on your own, and this life is yours to handle. You have to believe that something great will happen to you in the near future because, indeed, it will. In a way that shall surprise you! But you have to be ready for it! This is going to be good, and you will see something that has never been known or heard of before.

Why do you worry about what other people may say about you? Does it even matter that much? Clearly, it does not, and you know that better than anyone else, yet you still care! The fact of the matter is, nobody cares about your success or failure. Okay? Stop caring about what others may think or say about you. Savvy?

If you care about every little thing that others may say about you, you will never have a life left to live. The thing is, people can always find the faults in you, no matter what you do or how much you try to please them. You can't please everybody, so you shouldn't try.

This is a new life, and you should live a different way. You should remind yourself constantly on why you are who you are. You can't change that, can you? Stop trying to change yourself for others. Especially when nobody cares!

You came here alone, and you shall leave this place alone too. Nobody cares what you do as long as you do not hurt or harm anyone else in the process, under the standard of the law of the land, by the way. Nobody cares what you know! Nobody gives a damn!

If you want a better life, you should get a better solution for the problem that you're facing right now. The old solution is ineffective, and it is costly to keep.

Nobody cares about your sadness, so forget about everybody else. You are assigned to pass this test all by yourself. God is the examiner, so you do not have to prove it to anyone else but yourself and God. That's all you need to know. Pass the goddamn test, and move on. Shall we?

Nobody cares if you're the smartest person in the world. Nobody cares if you're a dimwit either. Simply, nobody gives a damn! Okay? So keep your mouth shut and work on your project. Make it happen, and have fun with it. Forget the naysayers because they don't matter much!

Involve nobody into your goal because it's personal to you, and only you can reach it. Your time is yours to control. Your life is yours to command. Your happiness is yours to create. Your peace of mind is yours to attain. You are the boss, and you are in charge, so you must be serious about it.

You are the boss of your life, and you have to work on and, for that matter, in it. In other words, you must work on the big parts as well as in the small details.

Be independent in your decisions. Be responsible for what you have decided to do. Be courageous in your thoughts, words, and actions. Freedom is attained through courage, responsibility, and independence.

NOBODY CARES

Your life will transform in many ways, mentally, physically, emotionally, and spiritually. In each step, you should take advantage of its result. Many of us had missed the opportunities in doing so when we were young because we didn't know the difference. Now it's a different time.

Limiting & Upgrading

When you were young, you thought that you were weak. When you get older, that same belief grows with you, and it gets bigger and more influential in your mind. Your self-esteem is low because your self-limited belief is growing bigger by the day. By and by, you're led to think that you can never get out of this life. You are trapped in one place, and you are helpless against this self-limited belief.

One thing you must be very clear: You must always aim at being better than your old self. That old version is no longer good for you. Get rid of it, and throw it away. You can upgrade now. Nobody has the rights to stop you from upgrading yourself, and nobody cares to do so either. Stop limiting yourself; start upgrading!

Chapter 7
The Comparison
When I Was Young

When I was young, I had a different idea about life and how to live it. Now things have changed. A lot of them, actually. For better or for worse, most ideas which used to ring true to my ears no longer seem to be relevant at this point, and my attitude toward them is no different than a cat to cake. My cat Tony doesn't like cake; it doesn't move Tony at all. Similarly, those old ideas are not as important as they used to sound. I did not really believe it at first, but I have grown up and, at the same time, outgrown those childish things too.

Comparison

The world we live in today is a competitive world, and we can't go on in life without any comparison, despite the fact that you hate it when somebody compares you with others. Especially the people who are close to you. For example, your friend is the subject of comparison. You are not happy when your mom keeps saying: *"Why can't you just be like your friend?"*

You can't stand it, and you want your mother to stop comparing, but you are too upset to say anything. Your mother takes it as a form of acceptance. She thinks that your silence has confirmed her belief. Wrong!

Nothing hurts you more than your mom's words of comparison, which are unfair and untrue. You don't want to respond because you're too hurt to say anything. You appear weak and wrong in her eyes! Although, in her heart, she loves you more than anyone else's kid, she still commits the one thing that no kid ever wants to witness, and that is to compare her kid with other kids. Again, and again! You want her to understand that you are not that dumb, but you can't say anything because you're too emotional.

Make Your Own Rules

You are convinced that the world may laugh at you when you make a fool of yourself. Whether you know it or not, it isn't true. The freaking world, in fact, doesn't give a damn about your downfall, nor does it really care about your triumph. In fact, nobody gives a damn about you or your life. Should you be upset that nobody cares? You should not! You shouldn't give a damn either. You have your own life to live. You make your own rules as you go along, as long as you don't break any laws, nor hurt anyone.

When your life seems like a lonely vessel floating through the sea of no-ending possibilities, whether for better or for worse, it is time to take full control of it, and make this life the most beautiful life, the way you want it, and the way you design it. Yeah, it may seem ugly at times, and you may feel like a fool, more times than you care to remember. You know what? You're growing stronger but better than ever before.

In short, the world doesn't give a damn about you or your life. Nobody does! But it gives you space and freedom to reshape your life and make it beautiful again. Most importantly, make it work for you again, rather than against your will. You're the boss, so be in charge. Nobody cares how you handle your life, and probably you shouldn't care about other people and how they handle theirs either. Fair enough? What? You don't care? Good!

Failures

I have failed more than enough to understand that not everything will go according to the plan. Life is supposed to be hard, and I'm supposed to fail a lot before I succeed. Does it mean I should never do what I want to do? No. Should I stop doing whatever that I'm doing? Not quite! What should I do? Even in the face of failures, I should persist and go on, for one day I shall succeed, and I shall be rewarded greatly.

You can fail, even in small things. And you might fail almost every day. Does it discourage you from trying harder? For most people, yeah, it does. But you, my friend, are different. You have a clear goal, and yeah, also a pair of blurry glasses. But you have a clear goal, so you should try harder even when you have failed many times. Don't be discouraged by those failures, for they are your teachers. Stingy teachers, I must say.

It's better to set a high standard for yourself and fail a few times before you succeed than to set a low standard and succeed in the first attempt.

When you feel down, I want you to remember two things: Why you feel down and how to get rid of this feeling.

Chapter 8
The Criticism
If you have never been...

You may fail many times before you can succeed.

Bad experiences can teach you better than the good ones.

If you know what you're doing, you'll succeed eventually.

Weak people criticize you for what they cannot do or accomplish. They envy your strength and they hate your guts.

If you never been wronged unfairly, you will never understand injustice.

If you have never been poor, you will not know what it's like to be desperate and helpless.

If you have never been judged unfavorably and unfairly, you will not treasure justice and fairness.

If you have never experienced defeat, you will be careless and reckless.

If you have never been short of money, you will not know how important it is to have enough of it.

If you have never been dumped by the one you loved, you will never truly understand the concept of heartbreak.

Keep That in Mind

You can't keep everyone silent from their part because they have every right to speak out even though you should not let those thoughts ruin your day or your peace of mind. Keep that in mind!

Your journey is yours to take. Nobody else has to care about it because it's your concern. Let people worry about their own problems, and you worry about yours.

Nothing is more irritating than to hear the same crazy stuff from people around you because they have no idea what you are doing with your life. They just cannot stop! You don't have to try to change them, for they will never change. They just can't! Leave them alone, and focus on your work. That's all you should care about. Remember, nobody cares whether you fail or succeed. Okay? In the end, you and you alone have to take the responsibility for your decisions and actions. Nobody else but you!

Before you know it, most people who criticize or complain about you will move on. In other words, they have completely forgotten you because they do not care about you or your life. Just remember that fact!

Why should you take their opinions seriously? They don't even know who you really are. Why do you even try to please them? They don't deserve your time or attention, and you know that.

Confidence

I was not confident about myself because my look had been successful in making the impression that I was nerdy and dumb. The crazy thing was that people believed it. When more people thought or even spoke to you as if you were dumb, soon enough you grew more convinced that you were dumb even when, in fact, you were smart. That was my reality in high school because I was not interested in looking handsome or sharp like other guys. In other words, how I dressed was the opposite of how I thought.

That begs the questions: How many high-school kids out there who feel the way I did?

I bet there are many. Some of them are unlucky with friendship. They are not good at expressing themselves through their look even though they are smart and cool (inside their heart). I hope this book can change their mind a little bit. Just a little bit! The title itself should remind them that, five years from now, nobody will care how you looked when you were a high school kid. They will see you in a different way and some of them may try to copy from you too. Been there, done that.

Confidence is the quality from within. If you have it, use it to your advantage. If you don't possess it, then create some because you can. How to be confident? It's a difficult question, but the answer remains the same: Confidence is a choice, not chance! It comes from the inside, not the other way around. But you must decide to embrace it.

At first, it would feel awkward, if not impossible. However, time shall take away any inconvenient doubts, including self-doubt, of course. Self-belief, on the other hand, is the key to build confidence. If you believe in yourself, you will make it happen. If you don't believe in your ability to change things around you, you won't make it happen, and confidence will remain absent, still.

If I've learned anything about self-confidence, I've learned this: Every decision that you make does count. People whose freewill is weak cannot stick to their words, nor actions because those words or actions are the products of the happenstances outside of their control. If you ask them to do something, for example, they may say yes if it benefits them. If it gets harder and harder, they would simply quit it and offer you nothing but a good excuse.

At first glance, self-confidence and a strong freewill may seem like irrelevant things, but when you look closely, you'll see the connection. If your freewill is strong, it can build strong discipline which will develop into a habit. A good habit! It's hard to create, but once it has been created, it will serve you well.

For example, you have decided to go to the gym, out of freewill, and you go. It has become the discipline to hit the gym regularly. Soon enough this discipline has become a habit, which is easy to follow once it's in place. As a result, you have become a gym goer, and you are confident about it, because you know you can do it and commit to doing it regularly.

Chapter 9
The Fears
Before 30 Years Old

I had lived with my parents (in my hometown), for 15 years until I moved to live with my aunt and uncle-in-law in the city Phnom Penh to continue my study, in the 10th grade. I arrived in November of 2008, and I had to wait for one month before I could finally get enrolled into the new school.

I learned that people were running fast in work, study, and in life, every day, whether they liked it or not. In the countryside, things were much slower and more predictable. In the city, everything was anything but predictable. You had to work fast if you ever wanted to make a good living in the city. You had to rely on your ability to do the job, and you were supposed to do it well. Otherwise, nobody would care.

I understood the challenges and fears clearly, given the fact that I had been keeping these fears with me for more than ten years. They were thought to be scary until I had come to the realization that if you get stuck with fears, you won't be able to do anything.

If you choose to do something despite your fears, you might as well overcome some of them. You can do what you want to do, regardless of how many fears that are standing in your way. You are strong enough to face those fears head-on and fight against them. At first, you might have felt that you were too small and those fears were too enormous and scary.

DARA LY

Before long, you could see that they were only made to look scary because you allowed them to look that way, due to the small mind that was in charge of your life, for many long years. In other words, fears only appeared big when you felt small.

You can reverse that, and you can overcome those fears if you only believe in yourself and trust that you can do what you want to do, with strong determination and discipline. You can do that without concern or worry about what might come next. Let the future worry about what might come next. All you should do is work hard now and be the best version of yourself.

After 30 Years Old

Honestly, I wish I could have had someone who would tell me that, but I wasn't that lucky. Still, I had managed to do just fine, and I had paid a fair price to pass the test and get ahead in life. For the first few years in the city, I did not know enough people; I was not well-informed about the situations and everything that took place. I was floating with time, waiting for the right opportunity to prove myself. I wanted to prove that I did have a real potential to do something that could matter in a big way. But time was a stingy friend, for all it gave me was cluelessness. Not to mention hardships!

If I had allowed time to rule my life, I wouldn't have made anything good or significant in this life before the age of 30 years old. In other words, if I had gone easy on my time, I would have wasted my life completely and unknowingly, to the point of no turning back.

Education was the key to a bright future. I took it seriously then, and I take it seriously now. This is why I write many books for young people, to remind them that they can and should do more for themselves if they ever want to make a name for themselves in this world.

To achieve such a high level of greatness, they must be fearless. In other words, bravery and courage shall bring you victory and triumph. Learn to be strong and fight hard for your life. You shall be successful. Worry no more about what others may think of you. Those people do not live your life; you do!

Another thing that I have learned is: Hard work!

DARA LY

My parents work hard all their lives, and the idea of hard work has been instilled in me and my siblings too, I believe. From there, I never have to force myself to try to work. Simply, my parents have done the job so well in forcing all their children to accept the philosophy of hard work through their examples. They didn't literally force me, my brother, and sisters. However, having watched them working from dawn to dusk, we all understood that we had our roles to help at home, and those roles were the tasks that we did, voluntarily or by assignment from our parents.

Now that I am better educated and well-informed, enough to get myself started in my career as an educator as well as a writer, I believe I can do more for other people whose direction of life has been unclear and blurry. I believe I can inspire them to do something that they have always dreamed of doing, and I want to save their time. They don't have to wait till they are 30 years old just to start doing something real and impactful.

I shall remind as many young people as possible. That's my job!

Chapter 10
The Reminding Random Reminders

Stop demanding attention from anyone else. That also includes the loved ones because they will not have such an idea of what you want. Stop it!

You either keep your life to yourself or you will be disappointed with the fact that nobody cares about your life. Nobody but you!

Manage your life and your time. Do not let time slip away easily. You have a big goal to get. You can't afford to be complacent.

Pick yourself up once again if you fall. It's not a big deal, and you are strong enough.

Worry no more about what other people are doing with their projects. You have your own business to run.

Don't be afraid to take charge. Don't be discouraged by the temporary setbacks. Give yourself enough time to deal with them one by one. Those setbacks are only for the time being, and you should overcome them all in no time.

You hold the key to your happiness. Nobody else can take that away from you without your permission. Nobody else cares about your happiness more than you do, and you know that.

Slowly but clearly, you are walking toward success. It's getting closer and closer.

DARA LY

You were born for great things, and God will remind you when you get complacent with the things that you're supposed to do and complete.

There are times when you need unlimited amount of patience, and there are times when you need great level of quickness. You alone will decide when and where to pick what.

Find peace in your work. Find peace in the process. Always know that you can upgrade and improve more. Never stay the same. Don't be too comfortable with your current results.

When you are feeling down, just remember: You're not a tree. You can reverse it.

You have to believe that great things will happen to you in the near future. Ignore the bad things. You must train your mind to ignore them.

A strong mind needs a strong body also. A strong body is the result of a high level of discipline.

I have never been more at peace at this point, although it is still limited to my need.

The difference between a carefree person and dramatic person is: Caring! A carefree person couldn't care less about the things that are not related to him while the dramatic one may find it hard to ignore almost everything.

You are on your own, in life, and nobody will be there to raise you up when you fall down. Nobody cares about your life and your work. It's you against you.

Why care too much about what you lost? It's the thing that you can't change because it's random and beyond your control.

Challenge yourself to the limit, and always find a new way to break it. It stands there only to test your will and strength. Use them both to break the limit, and be free as you wish.

NOBODY CARES

Nobody cares about your life and how you live it as long as you do not harm anyone else in the process. In other words, if you're a good citizen and respect others, they will leave you alone.

Control your time and your tasks. Do not let anything ruin your plan for the future. You've been working hard for it. Now it's time to reap the rewards.

Don't be too sure about the future that is beyond your calculation. It can be good or it can be bad, but you have to prepare for the worst thing that might happen also.

In the end, you are on your own, and you will rely on yourself rather than others. Nobody will be there to help you. In fact, nobody cares about you or your life.

Stop running away from your destiny. Get yourself together and do the job that you're supposed to do. No more excuses! No more delays.

Don't ignore the problems. Deal with them when you can. Fix them if you must. But don't ignore them!

I have grown to understand one thing about my work: Resisting is the key to getting the job done. When it gets tough, I resist the temptation of quitting.

Fight back against anything that is placed in your way. You must be tired, yes, but you can't let it stop you. You're almost there, and you should keep on. Don't quit! Don't give up!

There is a way you can go, and it is the path that you build by yourself. Don't walk with the crowd if you know they have different purposes and goals. Walk alone if you have to, but don't be afraid.

Don't worry about the future because it shall take care of itself. Don't worry about people around you; they know how to take care of themselves with or without you. Don't worry; start doing what you're sent to do on this planet. Simple enough?

You are strong enough to fight back. Don't let life treat you like garbage. You're the diamond, and your job is to polish it.

You are the boss, and nobody can and should talk you out of this life. Nobody can boss you around, so to speak.

Be yourself, and be unique in what you express.

One more thing, ignore the naysayers.

PART 2
FIND THE SOLUTIONS

Chapter 11
Time
Your Time Is Limited

You have to believe that something good will happen to you. To make it happen, you're going to need a lot of work done. Time is of the essence. You can't afford to waste any more of it. Your time is valuable, and to waste it for other people is not advisable. Now get to work to reach your dream faster. Don't delay any longer. The time is now, and you should start from here.

Use all your time to do your work instead of wasting it with people who see no value, nor value no words that have been promised. It's an insult, and you can't low down your standard just because these people are your friends. You are wasting your valuable time. From now on, get serious about everything that you do. It's a long way to reach the top, but don't be discouraged by that. Walk to your goal. Run when you have to, but don't stop, nor delay.

Your time is limited, but, quite often, you pretend that you have unlimited amount of time. That's why you keep delaying and delaying. Are you tired of delaying? You have to do something about it because delaying is not helpful at all. You do not want to regret it, right? Maybe it's time to stop delaying your work. It starts from today!

You have to be strict with your work and your time if you want to produce the best result. Get serious about what you think, speak, and act. Do what you say you would do. Do not

NOBODY CARES

think about what you don't want to do. Especially if those are useless things.

Things like these are all over the place, and one of your main responsibilities is to get rid of them from your life. By the way, you never needed them in the first place, so you don't have to keep them now or ever. Get rid of these unnecessary things from your life, and focus only on what you need and must have.

You can never be wrong on what you love. You can only be wrong if you do what you do not love, or maybe you do not love it enough. It's time to put down childish ideas and pick up what you should have right now. It's time to grow up and be successful. Start working on the project that you have been dreaming of achieving.

Learn everything you could about it, however long it may take. Believe me, it takes a lot of time to get it right. For the first few years, it's not easy, and, clearly, you would make many mistakes, big and small alike.

You might get confused more times than you care to count. Sometimes you might think about *Plan B*, meaning that you want to find a way out. In other words, you want to quit too soon. You shouldn't! You will get to the place you've been aiming for if you don't quit. Just make sure you get rid of the loser mentality in you. Get that loser out!

You might have had so many goals and dreams a few years ago, but most of them are just childish things, and you don't need them any longer. You should get rid of these childish goals for good because they are only distractions. Instead, focus on things that matter more.

DARA LY

Only you know what you want at this point; you have to be serious about getting them. There's no time to waste, and you must focus only on what you want.

Be Very Selective

Be very selective with the things that you need or want. Don't just choose everything that comes your way. It is not advisable, and you should get smart about what you choose because it involves you and your time.

Time is the most expensive commodity, so stop pretending that you have so much of it that you can spare or waste it with things that don't mean much to you. You will find countless of them along the way, and you might as well think about getting some of them. It's tempting, and, for an untrained mind, it is easy to fall into the trap of things which disguise as the so-called opportunities.

In contrast, your life will get slowed down because of the wrong choices you make about your time and what you do with it. Now it is obvious, and you won't need to worry about difficult choices.

There are only two options: **To be serious about your time or to take it easy**.

Your choice! If you want an easy life, you should be serious about your time and be strict when it comes to what you must do or want to do. On the other hand, if you want a difficult life, you won't need to be serious about your time. You'll get a life that gives you nothing but problems!

Stop Delaying

How many times have you delayed your plan because the timing is not right? Not right for what? For whom? Clearly, that is your excuse for not doing what you are supposed to do because you are not that serious about that goal. It's not your fault that luck doesn't choose you, but it is your responsibility to create luck for yourself so that you won't have to delay your plan.

If you get serious about your time and stop delaying, you will see that the timing has always been right. The thing that was not right was your belief. You did not believe that you could have made it a few years ago due to some invented excuses.

A task that needs to be done today must be done today. A task delayed for the next day is the task of tomorrow, and it doesn't count as today's task at all. In other words, because you keep it till the next day, that means you have accomplished nothing today. When you achieve nothing today, that means you have nothing. Frankly speaking, that's how I feel when I delay my tasks.

It's better to do something and fail rather than to do nothing and remain a nobody. If you want to remain a nobody, keep delaying your tasks and keep being a mediocre person. If you want a good result today, work today. Not tomorrow. Let the goddamn tomorrow take care of itself. You can't find an excuse for delaying.

Chapter 12
Work
To Leave or to Stay

Whenever you lose hope in yourself or get lost in life, remember this: Google can help!

Okay, maybe it can't. But when you lose sight of your purpose, or get lost in the middle of the journey, you should go back to the drawing board and see why you started it in the first place.

When it comes to your workplace and the people you work with, it's a complicated situation because you can't just leave this place or the people whom you consider friends. Maybe you will regret it later if you find out that the new place is worse than the one you want to leave. However, it's still uncertain for now because you're still here, and you're indecisive, whether to leave or to stay. That begs the question: Why do you want to quit this job?

Is it your boss that is unreasonable? Is it your coworker who wants to make your life more difficult? Or else?

If you cannot find the right reason to quit, that means you're not sure yet. In that case, I suggest you stay! At least, for a while. If you still don't like it, you can quit later.

Motivation for Work

What's the difference between your study and job? The difference is, you pay to learn in school while in the workplace, you get paid to learn. What's the similarity between your study and work? Well, if you fail, you fail; that's the similarity. It's frightening for the first few weeks or even months, right? You have many sleepless weekends while, on weekdays, you can barely open your eyes when you arrive home at the end of the day. The point is, you are scared because you care. You care about your performance. It's good.

Before you get a job, all you worry about is how to get one. After you've got one, all you care about is how to do it well. When you fail a few times for the first few weeks, you start doubting yourself and lose confidence in your ability to handle the job.

When you're in university, you want to get a job so that you can earn some money to support yourself. After getting a job and having little time left for self-study, you begin to question your previous decision on getting a job while in university. You need advice from anyone you could ask. The next day, you ask your classmates who happen to be jobless after quitting a few times from a few companies. What's the advice? Nobody cares about your job or your study, so you'll get an answer that you seek.

It's like asking a mirror if you look like Taylor Swift. Of course, you'll look like Tey-Ler because that's what your friends keep calling you! Tey-Ler!

NOBODY CARES

The point is, you'll get what you seek. You'll see what you believe because believing is seeing!

As a student, your job is to learn everything you could to prepare yourself for future career. When you finally get a job in a company, the real jobs you do are to learn and work at the same time. Actually, it's more like one job; you learn a specific skill so that you can do it well in that company where you're working.

When I started my very first job, I didn't know that I was supposed to deliver a presentation to the client, in English. I didn't know that, instead of assisting my team leader, I had to play the leading role in the discussion. I didn't know any of that, yet I had to adapt.

My number one fear in the workplace was speaking. The problem was, I knew next to nothing about the technical stuff. In fact, I could speak brilliantly, but I just didn't know about that yet. It took me a few weeks to find out.

From the beginning, it's not always smooth. In fact, it's difficult, especially when the tasks are tough, or even worse, soul-sickening. You often think about quitting it because, at least, it would be easier than to work. You are disappointed with your performance, yet you are clueless on how to improve it. Fear has dominated your mind almost every day!

When you improve your performance, your fear will automatically disappear. That's when your confidence is being regained. But you should rethink the way you work, and work hard to regain your confidence. The best way to be confident in your work is hard work.

Be as focused as you can be. Be disciplined. Many challenges can and will be overcome through focus and discipline. Each day, you save the reward in the working deposit.

If you are skillful in your job, you'll get through your day like sleeping. The day will be less stressed. If you don't like it, it'll be a long and tough day. It can be very stressful when you don't like it. You try to do everything just to avoid it.

You should think of long-term goal but focus on short-term details. It's a daily task to keep engaging with the details of your work. But you need to have a good system to track and measure the progress. If you just work in it, and not on it, soon enough, it'll control you, and you may end up getting lost in the details. It happens to many people who work but don't have a proper working system to control it. In turn, the work has controlled them.

Pay attention to the small details because they are the indicators of working progress. Without any way of measuring your progress, it's just hard to predict your next step.

Are you a detail-oriented person? How do you measure your progress each day? You need a system of measuring it if you want to improve faster. The system of measuring doesn't have to be complex. It should be easy to measure and practical in terms of accuracy.

Personally, I like something simple and easy to count. If I cannot count my progress, I don't know how to measure it. That's me! I keep as many records of my work as possible because I'm a big believer in recording. Numbers are my best friends in my work. Counting is our interaction. As much as I love my results, counting is the first love that I cherish.

I would say that I'm good with numbers because I love most of them. I love counting them, and I fantasize the thrill of seeing big number in whatever that I do. I don't do well if I can't count the numbers of the things or projects that I'm working on.

I do the same thing with finance. If I can't count my money, I consider it a failure in making money. If I can count and keep increasing more of it, that's a good sign for my financial balance.

There is no limitation in self-development, but without any work added to it, you can't get anywhere either. Realistically speaking, one should start from a small step and improve continuously to get to the next step, bigger and more challenging as usual.

Set a standard for yourself and work toward it. However, you have to calculate the costs and benefits too. You can't go in blindly and hope that everything will work out well. Sorry, but that's just not practical. It's not going to work that way, despite how much you want it to be true.

It is hard and tiring, of course, but it is hard work that builds a strong character and confidence in you. If you want to remain weak and less confident, you can skip this part. Well, perhaps, you can skip the whole book.

Even though you have just begun your journey in a company, you are not completely new to it. In fact, you can use your skills and what you've got to apply into the job and perform the best you can.

When it comes to working environment, it's outside of your control. Just like your classmates, you don't get to choose who your coworkers will be, nor can you decide who your boss is. However, you can choose the right attitude toward them, and work cooperatively.

Do Not Get Too Comfortable

Do not get too comfortable with your current life because it has not been fulfilled just yet even though, on the surface, it looks like you are making progress. It is much smaller compared to what you will have when your life is finally fulfilled.

Find the right place to work. If you haven't found it yet, keep looking. Don't settle for a place that does not allow you to improve and grow. Be flexible if you need to be. You should invest your time to improve your life and better your skills in a company that you work for. There is no limitation on how much you can grow and how far you can go. Regardless, you won't get anywhere either if you refuse to work hard or learn more. Period!

Chapter 13
Mindset
The World Is Not Always Fair

The world is not always fair, and you can't always complain about how unfair it has treated you. Do you know why? Because it has treated random people unfairly too, so you're not the only one who has to go through that, and you should stop complaining about useless things. It won't help at all, and you know that, so you should keep your mouth shut and concern yourself no more.

Just because the world is unfair to you, that doesn't mean you can't fight back to get what you want. You can and you should because it's the right thing to do. You are capable of doing anything that you want to do if you're passionate enough about it.

Be patient and stay strong, for the journey ahead is not over yet. It's a long road.

Discipline

Discipline can be obtained from repetition of good practices. A good practice starts from a choice, not chance! Don't rely on a chance because it will get you nowhere. In other words, don't wait for a perfect time to start doing something because a perfect time is as rare as a UFO sighting, if such a thing is real at all.

Balance

Time goes slowly when you're going fast. It goes fast when you're slow in motion. Time and action are connected in a perfect balance, and man controls this balance. When man is unaware of that fact, he is being dictated, if not controlled, by this balance.

We may not have control over things around us, but we can control ourselves from doing things that are embarrassing. Getting drunk is one example, and an easy one to point out. Bragging is another one. However, an unintentional error should not be considered an embarrassing issue because everybody makes mistakes. If you have done so, here is a piece of advice: Relax! Nobody cares! Period!

Be the Winner

You used to be in that rough situation and struggling to make ends meet. But now things have to change, and you must adapt to these changes if you wish to be where you want to be. Get used to being new and different from who you used to be. The life as a loser is long gone, and you know that. You used to run away from your own greatness because you never believed in your heart that it was what you deserved.

You deserve a great life because you work hard for this. Now it is time to reap the rewards. You don't need to delay anymore.

Don't believe what people are saying about you. They don't have a clue about your life and what you do, and there is no reason to get upset about the things that are untrue. Nobody cares about untruthful things. Get to work, and be the best you can be, and get the rewards that you deserve.

You are the winner, and you must get tough about what you do. You can't just let the opinions of others ruin your plan. You must be in charge of it.

Chapter 14
Freewill
Freedom

Freedom, a concept so abstract to many minds that it is hard to contemplate, is a gift granted by God to all men and women for that matter. But freedom is a natural right to all people, rich, or poor, educated, or illiterate, common, or elite. But freedom is only a tool, ready to be used. One must exercise it if he wishes to have it.

Nevertheless, there is a boundary between freedom and law, created by God also. One cannot exercise his freedom while violating the law and resulting in harm or sin against others. That's the hardest part about freedom. Freedom breeds power, wisdom, and strength, but in equal level, which is a fragile balance. Too much of power and too little wisdom will result in corruption. Too much wisdom with too little strength will result in vulnerability. Too much power with too little strength will result in destruction for others and oneself.

A free man has many opportunities to explore the possibilities that he can do or wants to do. He can manage his life better than people with little freedom in their lives. In some places, freedom is hard to find, and even harder to exercise. If you live in a place where freedom is fully appreciated and respected, you should consider yourself lucky.

Unfortunately for women, the freedom that men take for granted is largely absent. Something has to be changed, and it has to be made in a big way. First, it starts with a woman to lead the way. But who can do that? She can do it!

But who is she? She's a girl who has tasted the concept of freedom although it's still not enough. She has seen unfairness in the community, and she wants to change it. She wants to bring freedom to other people, men, and women alike.

She wants to show the world that everyone is equal in the eyes of God, and no one should be stripped off his or her freedom. She has a mission in life, and it is to bring freedom to all men and women in the world, through education.

It's a big mission, and almost impossible, but she believes in the power of God, and she believes in her freedom and freewill to do what God has empowered her to do.

If God is with her, what else can stand against her will? The devil? He won't stand a chance!

You Are the Boss

Do not let anyone influence your decision about your life and your future. To go fast or slow, it's entirely up to you to choose. Nobody should intervene in your decision-making process. Only you should take a full responsibility for your life and your success. If one thing does not go according to your plan, you should take the responsibility. If you make a mistake, you should take the responsibility. No need to rely on anyone else!

You are here to do great things, and you must take your time seriously. Don't waste any more time. You are the boss, so you must act like one. The time has come that you must embrace your true nature. You are the master of your own fate, and you must not let anyone else do the job for you. Take control of your life, and be the boss.

Don't worry about the future. It shall take care of itself. But you need to focus on your present and what you're doing right now. Don't let time slip away easily.

You can't rely on someone else's approval for what you want to achieve. You must do it, whether people approve of it or not. That's not your concern. You must do what you must do if you want to get your job done. Nothing else matters at this point, and you know that too. If you wait for someone to agree with you before you do something, you'll be a loser because only a loser would wait for approval from someone who has no idea what's at stake. You don't have to agree with me, but you can try and see for yourself. Own your life, or someone else will. Do the best you can today, or you'll regret it later. Surely, you don't want to regret it, do you?

DARA LY

You can't take the whole burdens to yourself alone. You need to know how to delegate and manage your life and everything that goes around. You can't be doing all things for everyone all the time. It's not going to work out well for you, and you know that. Stop trying to solve everyone else's problems. You've got a life to live. Don't you ever forget that!

If you know that you're doing the right things for your family, there is nothing you should apologize for. You either work hard now while you still have what it takes, or you will grow old and weak at one point. You don't have to listen to me, though.

You should listen to your heart, and hear what it has to say. Hear that? The yearning for freedom to choose and do what you desire to do. The greatness inside of you that keeps screaming from the depth of the dark place. Now it is time to free the beast in you.

You are the boss, so you do what you must do. Don't let anyone else tell you otherwise. Or you will forever remain a loser. You are not a loser, so stop thinking or acting like one. Stop it from now! You can't afford to think or act like a loser from now on because you are the winner and the master of your own life.

Chapter 15
Independence Planning

Your life is dictated largely by planning. Personally, I plan most of what I do for my work, even if I never reveal the plans to anyone else. The thing is, some of those plans are over-optimistic, at best, and absurd, at worst. When I read some of them, I want to laugh at myself for being such a naive yet supremely confident person who thought anything could be possible the way he wished. I still believe it even if I haven't been able to prove my case just yet.

Planning is good, but wishful thinking is not. Calculation serves the best interest of the planner, but errors or biases are usually the barriers of good planning. You can't manage to get the best plan out of your head if it is full of clouded feelings or, even worse, biases. More often than not, the place has a huge impact on how good a plan can be. A good place shall allow good thoughts and ideas to take root. A bad place, on the other hand, will drain your energy continuously in ways that won't allow a good plan to be planned.

Big Pictures & Details

Whatever you choose to do is the future that will manifest in your life. You may have to sacrifice some of your old habits to achieve new things in the future.

The work itself is the reward if you enjoy doing it every day. In contrast, it will be a tough time if you are being dictated by the details instead of being in charge of the whole operation.

Having said that, big pictures and details should go hand in hand if success is to be realized. In an operation, you need to know where to start and where to finish; those are the big pictures of the project. Along the way, you need to know how to fix problems when they occur, whether according to the plan or not.

To become independent in your work or whatever you do, you have to see the big pictures and know how to manage the details.

The World Doesn't Owe You Anything

The world doesn't owe you anything. Nobody else does! And you're not a victim! You're in charge of your destiny and happiness. Be the boss and take control over your life. Be independent in your decision-making process, and be fully responsible for the outcome.

You may think that it's okay to blame someone else for your own misfortune or disappointment. Bad things can happen, and everyone is not immune to this happenstance. It is very random yet certainly saddening. However, people who refuse to be the victim will not be saddened by it longer than they should be. In other words, they are independent from sadness because they are in full control of their choices!

From teenage life to maturity, you'll be amazed by how much different your life can be from one stage to the next. You might have been loud or outspoken when you were younger, but it can change as you get older. You might be less expressive in terms of what you say, but the words that are being spoken could carry heavier meanings than before. Your thoughts are not as childish as they used to be when you are an adult because adults are no longer interested in childish issues. Adults are more independent and responsible in what they think, speak, and act.

Be the best you can. And do not settle for anything less. You have all the time you need to build the best body and the best mind you want. Do it. Don't be concerned over things that are irrelevant. You are the boss of your work and life. Do your job and take charge of your life. Take responsibilities for what you are doing. Don't make unnecessary excuses.

You don't need permission from anyone to do what you're dreaming of doing. Just take the time to do it. Afford all you can and work super hard. You'll get there faster than you thought. Sometimes you may fail, but that's okay. Without failure, one doesn't appreciate the importance of hard work.

You'll succeed someday, if you work harder. I wish I could say the opposite. Don't be discouraged by failure, for it is only the lesson that you need to learn and overcome. Don't ask for help if you can do it by yourself. Do it yourself first. You want to be independent, right? Just do it!

There is a fine line between relying on someone else and doing it all by yourself before asking for help. You know what you can do and what you can't.

Be independent!

Be responsible!

Be free!

Chapter 16
Courage
Fear

Inspiration comes from everything that you see if you open your mind to receive it. When you feel motivated to do something, that's when your inspiration sparks the flow of new ideas, or in some cases, better ones. Needless to say, it comes with some forms of fears that you may have carried with yourself. Normally, these fears do not disturb you when you're inactive in that particular area.

When you review that area, the fears immediately emerge from somewhere. In fact, we deal with them continuously. Your mind is far stronger than you thought because it can deal with a lot of problems, which were previously considered to be unsolvable. However, without a proper training, the same mind is useless and powerless against many obstacles, especially fears. That begs the question: How to train your mind to be strong enough to fight against fears?

Fears come from irrational feelings or evidences of things that are familiar to the mind, but often projected as bad or scary, regardless of the truth. The mind is led to react to these irrational feelings by producing fears. They are fed by similar stuff each day, and soon enough, they become more real than before.

Another way to deal with irrational fears is to ignore them for as long as you can. To make that possible, you should refocus your attention on something else that is completely opposite of what you fear. Be it your job, success, happiness, or health.

At first, it's uncomfortable, but you'll get used to it and know how to deal with this discomfort properly. It might take some time, but it will get easier. To ignore fears doesn't mean that you know they're absent; it just means that you learn to live with the fact that fears do exist in your mind, based on habitual patterns.

How to Be the Best

If you want to be the best, you must study from the best in your field, or even those from slightly relevant fields. When you get deep into the field, you ought to see what the public could not. Every small detail does count and can help you understand better. Even a crazy story will someday make a good recipe for success.

Get deep into your field and dig everything you can. You'll see what you missed in the first place. If you want to be the best, you have to train hard every single day. You can't afford to take a break even one day. That's the truth about being the best.

You can do what you want to do when you put your mind and heart into it. But it's not always easy, especially from the starting point. You must outwork and outsmart your obstacles. No time for party. No time for slacking off. No time to waste. Focus on your work and be the best. Stay at the top.

Be tough and don't settle for less. You are built to be the best, and nothing less. Beat all the best in your world, and be the winner. Stay there, and never come down. The latter is the hardest part, so to speak, but you can do it. You have to be fast and be well-calculative. You have the same amount of time, but you can make more if you work fast and work right. Both have to go hand in hand because with the absence of one, your work will be imbalanced.

You are free to be the best if you choose it and embrace the lifestyle. But it is a lonely life, if you will. Learn the mentality of the best people, and see if it suits your thinking system naturally. If it doesn't, reinvent your system, or upgrade it by habitual reinforcement.

You have to know what you want, or you will remain, at best, an average person, or, at worst, a mediocre person. A mediocre person is the generalist who knows about too many things but very little and not enough to be able to use such knowledge to make anything. The good news is, there are many generalists this world can produce; they are everywhere because they are being taught that way.

The experts are very few and rare, but these few brilliant minds have created so many things that the generalists could never make. There is a fine line between the two types, and it is separated unmistakably by the mindset.

Anyone who wants to be the best or expert, for that matter, can become the best if he or she chooses the right mindset for the job or project that he or she is taking. With that being said, it's not easy to be the best. If it was, everyone would be doing it already.

The fact is, it takes a unique kind of person to become the best. He may not get along well with most people he comes into contact with. He may not like many things that many people do. He may not laugh at the jokes that most people would. He has a different way of thinking, and he acts according to his personal conviction, regardless of the circumstances.

Chapter 17
Control
No Need to Rush

No need to rush for anything, for you had always rushed in your entire life, and nothing worthwhile had happened just yet. You have no reason to be impatient right now, so no need to rush.

You will get what you want, and you will have what you deserve. All you need to do is work hard each and every day. Do the best you can with everything you've got. One day you will have what you're aiming for.

In this world, you can't have what you want all the time, but you can have what you've earned every single time. It never fails!

Every day we question ourselves whether we have what it takes to be who we want to be in the future. Don't worry about tomorrow because it can and will take care of itself.

At Home

You can be smart and hard-working, but you won't get out of poverty circle if you let family distract or slow you down from what you're doing. Maybe you won't believe me when I tell you that your family can be very distracting if you don't explain yourself clearly enough.

It happens a lot to entrepreneurs who have just begun the journey in this business world. You're one of them now, so you ought to deal with it in a fair manner, or you'll be forever trapped in the middle of your family and business.

Life is not always easy when you let people stand in the way. Especially when those people are very close to you. As painful as it sounds, your loved ones are not always supportive, nor do they know what you're doing with your life and everything that's going on in your work.

You have to set a clear boundary so that people will know what to expect from you. It's nothing personal, though. It's just business, and you know that, but they don't, so your job is to explain to them what's at stake. Otherwise, you'll be living in a miserable life, trying to breathe in the middle of two opposite sides: **Your family and your work!**

When your family is not on the same page with you, it's hard to keep a good life balance between work and family. Many successful businesspeople have failed in this attempt for many reasons, but one of them is misunderstanding! Time is yet another factor!

At Work

At work, it's important to maintain respect among your colleagues. Respect is everything, and it is demanded by and from everyone, including yourself. You must respect everyone else the way you want to be respected. With fairness, it is possible; without it, it is hardly the case, if not impossible.

If you want people to respect you, you must earn it. The way to do so is hard work. The results shall speak for you, and that's when respect has been earned. But you have to be fair and honest about that. Don't just pretend that you're working hard while you're not. Don't promise what you can't do, in the workplace. Don't brag about anything that you haven't achieved yet. It's only a joke if people find out about that.

Never ever allow anyone to convince you that you're less than good. Stand your ground and be open about what you're standing for. There is nothing to apologize for if you're doing the right thing and being fair.

Remember: Nobody cares if you're right or wrong, but you have to prove that you are right.

You have to believe in yourself even when nobody else does. Nobody else knows your capability better than you do, and nobody else has the authority to convince you otherwise.

Believe in your ability and work hard to back it up. Of course, you will face challenges. Who hasn't? But those, who are bold enough to try one more time after each failure, will achieve the impossible result. It is only impossible before you have tried one more time, by the way.

The whole world may be convinced that you're not worthy of the success that you've been dreaming for, but you can't be led to believe so. The world does not care if you're worthy of success or not, but you have to prove that you own your future.

You're worthy of it! But first, you must be clear about what you want. Many people are unsure of what they want, and they end up failing at random goals. Don't fall into the same category. You're better than that!

Ignore the rest of the world. Focus on your goals and work hard to achieve them as soon as you can because you can never be too sure of the future and what might happen to you next. But one thing for certain is that you can achieve them faster if you work harder now.

Fair enough?

Stay Silent

People can misjudge you or look down on you. You can't stop anyone from doing so. You can't expect everyone to know what you're up to because your goal belongs to one person only. That person is you, so don't waste your time telling people what you want to do. Keep your mouth shut and work to achieve your goal. Do we have a deal? Besides, nobody cares, anyway. Why waste your time talking about it?

You don't have to tell anyone what you're going to do. Just do it. Be silent if you must, but don't worry. You'll get there one way or another. It's better if you conserve your time and energy for the tasks, meaning that you should spend less time talking and more time doing your job. Agree?

People have the rights to judge or underestimate you, but you don't have any rights to do so to yourself. You have to believe in yourself because you're more powerful than you know. To unlock that power, you must keep working and practicing every day until you've found that hidden power. It's the power from within, only found through hard work and repetition of practices.

Stay silent and work hard every day. The power of silence is far more powerful than you know it. You'll see it when you get there. To get there, you must keep working harder and harder every day. I can't stress that enough.

You can live anywhere on this planet and still do what you're dreaming of accomplishing because the world is far more connected than it ever was. If the people from a few generations before us could achieve so many incredible things with little help of the connectivity level that today's world can provide, so will you.

Chapter 18
Decisiveness
Goals

People have different goals. Some want a good family. Some want to be rich. Some want to be broke. Okay, maybe the last one is rare. But the point is, different people have different ideas about how to live a good life, leading their choices to vary from one another. What about you? What are your goals?

You may have started later than others, but that doesn't matter because everyone has a different path in life. You walk your own way, and others walk theirs! There's no point in comparing your life with anyone else's unless it enhances your life in a positive way, which is quite rare, by the way. Besides, nobody cares about your goal, so you don't need to compare.

You have a potential to grow better in your work. But to make it happen, you must sacrifice a lot more than you think. The higher you get in this life, the more you can see, and that means your initial ideas about your life could have been inadequate. In other words, when you were younger, you were dumber. Now that you are more mature, you know better, and you can do better.

Balance

Build your mind with education and your body with exercise. Strengthen your soul with faith and your heart with love. Balance your life!

Walk alone for a while if you have to. Friendship is not a good recipe for growth, especially if your goal is different. Sometimes your friends might bring you down with them even if they don't mean to do so. It happens a lot in friendship. Balance your life, and keep your friendship in a healthy balance if permissible.

Don't let anyone stop you from doing something that you're passionate about. Perhaps, it will take more time than you planned, but your life is designed for this particular purpose, and you can afford it, but you have to have a perfect balance.

When you're busy with one thing, you tend to forget the other ones which are also important. That's when imbalance takes place, and as a result, you will find it hard to focus on anything. At least, not in a practical manner!

Balance is the key!

Patience

It pays to be patient with what you do, especially if that is a big project. Find a new way to get a better result, and never get too comfortable with the current one.

You don't need to show off your achievement to anyone unless you get paid to talk about it. Keep your mouth shut and work hard to get what you want. Don't tell anyone what you're up to because it's a waste of time. Stay calm and be patient!

Keep your mouth shut and be the best you can be. More important still, you must outwork your old self every day. Rest if you must, but never stop. That's the way to become better. You may feel frustrated when the pace that you go is slower than you expect, but you must also remember to calculate every move you make and each step you take.

Your goal is to be better than who you were.

Remember?

It takes some time, so be patient!

Having said that, you can have all the time you need in the world, but if you don't use it, you'll lose it. On the other hand, you might be very busy, but if you have a clear idea of what you want to do, you can always make time to complete it. Once again, patience is important!

Progress

Life is supposed to be hard sometimes. You're supposed to try your best in everything you do. Nobody will give anything that you haven't earned because nobody cares about you or your goal, for that matter. You have to earn it!

When your work is unpredictable, you're making progress. When you are clueless about what your next move is, you're making progress. In other words, it's new and it's exciting.

It's normal to be tired when you're in the middle of the road. Those who quit along the way will be forgotten; those who refuse to quit will be victorious. There's a price to pay. That begs the question: Can you pay for it?

Nobody will do that for you, and you know that. You have to pass the test by yourself. Be serious about it and be determined to get it done.

Interested or Not Interested

Every decision that you make should be determined by only two factors: **Interested** or **not interested**!

If you're interested in music class, go for it. If you're not interested in it, avoid it like your ex. Or exes! If you're interested in saving money, save it. If you're interested in spending it, it's your money. If you're not interested in learning math or chemistry, that's your choice but also your responsibility. If you're interested in math, go for it. It is as simple as that!

Just keep in mind that you are responsible for your own actions and decisions. It is your freedom to choose. With freedom to choose comes responsibility. You own it, and you have to take care of it. Your life is your choice and responsibility, so choose wisely.

Do not let this life drift in a random direction; you are in control of it. If it goes at a random direction, that means you are not doing a good job in managing your life. Do not let the random happenstances win over your life.

Chapter 19
System Upgrade
The Right Way

You can't find the right way to go when you try to find it with someone else. It's the path for one, and it can't be for more. You know that better than anyone else! Sometimes you need a new perspective on what you've been doing.

It's a long road, and only a few have succeeded so far. Now it's your turn. Will you make it? Only you can answer that. Only time can affirm it.

Your Life

When you want to give up on your life, just think of one thing: You'll come back again next life, so perhaps, it's wiser to learn everything you can now before departing this place too soon.

As you grow older and more mature, many things will become dull and boring. You no longer give a damn about what your friends say about you or what you do. You simply couldn't care less. And you're right about that because nobody cares about you more than you do.

Now you're on your own, and your life is free once since for all. You don't have to hurt yourself any more than you already have. The journey is far from over, and you ought to keep going.

This life is a long journey, and you know that. And get this: Nobody cares about your breakup stories. There's no point in talking about that, nor should you demand attention from anybody. Nobody cares!

Whether you're right or wrong, nobody cares. Whether you're good or bad, nobody cares. Whether you're sad or not, nobody gives a damn! Shut your mouth and stay quiet. Deal with your problems by yourself, and try not to involve others in the process because nobody gives a damn about you and your messed-up life. You're strong enough to handle it. Stop demanding others to care about your own life. You're the boss, and you alone have to take care of it. Fair enough?

You might find it hard to believe, but nobody cares about things that you are dealing with right now. Again, nobody gives a damn! Okay?

DARA LY

I've been dealing with the same issue, and I know that nobody gives a damn about my life. I've stopped trying to reverse it a long time ago. I simply live my own life, and I couldn't care less if anybody misunderstands my way of life. People have the rights to disagree. What else can I do to stop them? Nothing!

Plus, I wouldn't do that even if I could. I respect the differences of opinions from people, and I have my own too. As long as I don't break the law, I couldn't care less about the differences of opinions from others. Simply, I don't care!

It's my life, and I'm in charge.

Information

There are many things that you can do because you're still young, and you have the time to do what you deem necessary for the future.

It's not important where you start, but where you're going. You can start from anywhere. The proof of your ability to do things depends largely on the direction of your undertaking and how you manage it. It's not a pointless journey, however. It only seems so when you've lost the direction that you're going, at times, but as you resume your purpose, it shall be clear that it's the well-planned journey with well-equipped mindset.

There is a fine line between seeking information and accepting idea from people. If you treat everyone around you like mini-Google source, you'll find them useful in some ways. If you treat people like gods, you'll find it hard to reject their opinions or even misinformed ideas about things. Kids might believe a beautifully narrated lie from adults, but you are not a kid, so don't just take every word from everyone like it is the fact, without fact-checking it first. Fair enough?

For now, you keep watchful eyes on what is true and what is not, and be sure to double check before using it in your work, or for that matter, your life. For better or for worse, information can shift many things in the process, so be selective in what you get into your brain and the source of it. By that, I mean, be very selective. Period!

You need to deal with the fact that you may absorb a lot of useless information before you can get the good stuff. In this new world, where all kinds of information travel at the speed of light, one can never be too careful about what kind of information is good and should be taken seriously. Anybody can provide any kinds of garbage which would turn you dumber if you ever take them seriously, by the way. However, people are entitled to their rights to offer opinions as well as information as they see fit, and you, as a consumer of information, should be selective and smart about it, or you will be led to the wrong direction. As a result, you may waste a lot of valuable time. Not to mention energy and effort!

Chapter 20
Nothing and Nothing Maturity

What is it that you want right now? Are you inspired to do more and be more? Don't let the past failures stop you from doing better and being successful. Forget the naysayers. Forget the critics. Forget everybody else! Just focus on your work!

When you're stressed out about your study or work, just remind yourself one thing: "Because I can!" When you truly believe it, no obstacle is too big to overcome.

Maturity comes in many forms, but one that is more common than the rest is well-planned thinking. When your work aligns with your thinking, maturity will take place.

For a lengthy period, many things are not in the right places, and you couldn't be more frustrated with the messy situations. However, it is your job to rearrange them and put everything into the place where it belongs.

When you get more mature, fewer things can excite you. Neither can they scare you! Calculate your next moves carefully. Do not rely on wishful thinking. Pay attention to every aspect of your work. Do not overlook small things, for they can be the reasons your work fails.

Two Things You Should Care

There are two things you should care about: **Nothing and nothing!**

You're on your own, and nobody will come to your rescue. You have to rely on yourself and be responsible for your own decisions and actions. You can't worry too much about anything or anyone else. You can't stop anyone from doing anything that he or she wants and believes to be the right thing.

When it comes to money or success, I expect neither one. In fact, I don't expect anything right now. My life seems to go on the path of no expectation, which is weirder than it already has been.

If you care too much about too many things, you won't have peace of mind. You don't have to know what others may think or say about you, if you know you are doing the right things. People can say whatever they like; it's their freedom to speak even when they may say dumb things, at times.

As a Teenager

As a teenager, you are convinced, in some ways, that you have to prove your worth to the world. As you grow mature and deal with your life and work, in particular, you realize that nobody cares about what you do. Why would you try to prove or tell everyone about everything that you think or plan to do? That, to me, is a lame idea. I know, I sound like an arrogant person, but reality is the meanest yet truest teacher. I learned that thing the hard way. I come to the realization that nobody cares about my work or failures, and successes, for that matter. I don't need to prove my worth to anyone else, or even the world!

PART 3
THE TURNING POINT

Chapter 21
Value
The Valuable Lessons

You could be the best student or the most favorite one in the class back in the old days, but frankly, nobody cares now! Period. You might be wondering why nobody does. The reason is simple: "Nobody cares!" Okay, that doesn't sound like an answer, but the fact of the matter is, people are busy with many things, and they do not have time for others.

The world is full of drama and attention seeking actions, and many of us can be influenced, in some ways, by those things too. We are not completely immune to it because it's a far more connected world. However, we can shield off some bad influences from bad actions.

When you stop demanding everyone to be attentive to what you are doing, you'll find true freedom and peace. Most importantly, you'll find true and permanent happiness. However, it's hard to resist the temptation of attention seeking from the world around you. Especially when you have something to show people. I don't want to use the terms "show off," just so you understand.

When I was a kid, I always wanted my uncles to notice or acknowledge my presence. I wanted attention, if you want to know the truth. What a silly thing to do. But what did I know? I was just a kid. A countryside boy who was clueless about things outside the hometown! New people and new things never ceased to fascinate me.

DARA LY

As I grow older and become more aware of the world, I realize that it is childish and pointless. Again, this is merely an example. There are many things that are pointless, at this point, yet they used to dominate big part of your brain when you were younger. We all had been through those things. My only conclusion is this: "**Nobody cares about them anymore!**"

As a writer, I operate in the same mindset as a student. I study everything I can before I take the test. Each project is a test, and my goal is to hit the top score. I want to break old records in sales and commercial success. At the same time, I know one thing about people: Nobody cares if I fail or succeed. Thus, I will not waste any time concerning about what they have to say about me or my work.

People will forget about you sooner than you think. They will no longer remember the good things that you do. They don't give a damn about your shortcomings either. They simply don't have time or attention for that. Okay? Just remind yourself that! Nobody cares about your life, and you clearly don't give a damn about theirs either.

Stop caring whether others may care about you or not because nobody does. Nobody did, and nobody will! You'll find freedom and peace after you've realized this simple fact about people around you.

Does that mean you have to ignore most people in your life? Yeah! There are more people with nonsense stories than those who have the same respect for you the way you respect them. You should avoid the former and keep in touch with the latter although it will be a very limited connection.

Focus on what you can do now, and ignore what people say. They might not know your ability, and that's okay because they don't matter much at this point. Your work does. Your commitment does. Your focus does. People don't!

You need to be self-reliant and effective in whatever that you're doing if you want to be very successful in the field that you have chosen. The road ahead is uneven for the most parts, but it won't be a big deal because you can deal with all kinds of troubles that present themselves along the way.

Whatever that you do will define your result in the future. Do it with your heart and do it well. Don't go easy on yourself if you want the best result. Ignore the noises from everyone else around you. Focus on the values that you are providing.

Since I was young, I have relied on myself more than others. Maybe I'm just too lazy to ask for help from anyone else. Maybe I'm too busy to ask. Or simply, I don't need help from anyone else if I can do it myself.

Know Your Limits

There have to be some ways to get to where you want to be. Know your limits and try to break them as soon as you can. You are strong enough to win. You're a one-person army, and you are built for this purpose: Winning!

Ignore the temporary setbacks, and focus on the future ahead. Things shall go in accordance with your will if you refuse to yield. Only a loser would surrender to small obstacles. You are not a loser, so stop acting like one. Okay?

You are the winner, and the winner fights even when time gets tough. The winner refuses to surrender even under the most unbearable circumstances, which would take down a person whose spirit is weaker and heart is less committed. The winner will go all in even when it means life-and-death situation.

You either win or you keep fighting. The more you work on your work, the more you get to see why you are going to win. You just have to keep working and working until you get the job done and get it done properly.

You are neither perfect nor bad. You are in between perfection and imperfection. The gap is big enough, but your aim should be to get closer to being perfect because that's the area where many legends are made. Aim at being closer to perfection!

Believe in Yourself

You can't simply keep everything that people say in your head. The longer you keep, the longer it slows you down. You don't need anyone else's help. You can do it yourself. If nobody believes in you, you believe in yourself. You might fail now, but you will not lose if you refuse to give up. The road is rough from time to time, but do not quit. You are on the right path. You need to keep going. Keep doing it.

Do what you love and don't let anybody talk you out of it. You know that you are doing the right thing and you are helping more people. You owe explanation to yourself and God only. Others do not matter much!

You can't let anyone stop you from reaching your goal. You have to work hard and you have to be strong.

It's a long way from your goal. You must keep walking toward it and never look back. You have passed all the hard parts; now it's time to finish what you have started.

Obstacles shall present themselves along the way, but they will not stop you. People who oppose you will be there to try to stop you, but they will not stop you. You hold the key to your future.

Don't be discouraged by failures, for they are not permanent. You have to get up if you get knocked down. You have to fight for your future. Believe in yourself!

Chapter 22
Self-Development
If You Fail, You Fail

If you fail, you fail. Nobody cares! If you succeed, you succeed. Nobody cares. If your life is in a dark place, it's in a dark place. Nobody cares.

There is no point in comparing your current failure with your classmates or feel bad. Look at me, I've failed in my work more times than I care to count. I've grown up and become more mature, and I learn just one thing: **Nobody cares about my life and my work!** I alone have to take charge. But I will not go through my life being a victim of anything or circumstances.

I'm the boss. I answer to myself and God only!

No Excuse

It's just another ordinary day, and you don't have to have excuse for not working. You can be sick or unwell, but you can't make it as an excuse. You might find it hard to sit straight at the desk right now. So what? You have to work!

There are many ways you can get to your goals, but excuse is not one of them. Never make excuse and pretend to be upset after the result has gone bad. Never make excuse and overreact only after it's too late.

It's a long way from here to the finished line, and you will have to deal with many things unpleasant, if not heartbreaking or disappointing. It's a tough situation but you can overcome it eventually.

Every decision that you make does count. Every little detail that you do does contribute to your success. A switch of your action and thought could be a game-changing idea in your work.

No excuse!

Study

Nobody cares if you fail or succeed in your learning journey. It is entirely up to you to decide whether you want to fail or succeed. It might sound simple, but the reality couldn't be more unpleasant. You have to go through many nights without sleep so that you can review and memorize the lessons for the upcoming exam. Your parents want you to succeed, but they cannot do anything about that. Only you can do that.

Despite some challenges, you have to have strength and faith in yourself. Your family cannot help you forever, and you ought to get on your feet and do all the things that you are supposed to do. You don't have to wait.

Hit the books right now! Learn something! Treat your study seriously. Become better every day. You'll thank yourself, ten years from now on. When you get serious about your work and your time, everything is getting easier to manage.

Meanwhile, many things will have to be excluded from your daily life.

Reading

You get up and go to work. You get back home at the end of the day, with you head blank and your body tired. Your life is on auto-pilot mode for, at least, 5 days a week. Weekend might seem like a good time, but in reality, it's not. You have a difficult life. But you know what? Nobody cares. Period!

You are trapped in one place long enough to become convinced that there is no other way to get out of this place. There is one way to get out, and that is to read books. You always have choices. You may not know it yet, but you always do. More often than not, you are limited by your own mind because it lacks information. That's why you should read more if you want to find out more possibilities for the future.

Through reading, you will see beyond the current limitation that is blocking your mind. It will open your heart for new things. The things that were absent in the past.

Maybe you're too busy with your work. Maybe you have no time for reading. However, there is one way that can be a win-win solution. You should read the books that are related to your work.

Your brain is the most powerful tool, but it needs constant fuel to keep going. It needs special kind of food to produce great things. It needs reading!

Chapter 23
High Achiever
Hard Times

Remember this: Nothing in life is easy, as always. There will be times when things get harder than you thought they would or could. But tough times make a tough person, and they build your character for the better. You'll become stronger and wiser as you face hard times.

I know you hate tough times, but you don't hate them more than you're sick and tired of them. That's the truth. In fact, you have been strengthened by those hardships. For that, you should be grateful.

When I was young, my childhood wasn't always bright or colorful. But when it got dark, I played hide-and-seek with my cousins. That's how it went. I did not have the privilege to have fancy toys, which explains why I do not seem to need any of them right now. I did not have free time since my home was like a small factory which required all available hands to operate. I hated the additional tasks even though I did complete my assigned tasks. But it took almost all of my free time.

I would say that my childhood was a training field. I had learned just enough to survive anything that would come my way, no matter where I might go. All of this is possible because of hard times in my early childhood. What they did was strengthening me.

Reshape Your Life

Nobody cares about what you know unless you have created something that can benefit other people. You have chosen a different path from most people in the world, so you don't have to complain about it. You can't compare your life with them either because they work for others while you work for yourself.

Nobody cares about what you do if you do not produce a concrete result. Ignore the rest of the world for a while. You have a project to complete. A business to run. A life to fulfill! Reshape your life the way you want. Do not listen to the naysayers; they don't know what they're talking about. You don't have to be afraid to do what you are sent to do in this life.

You Are on Your Own

Nobody cares if you are suffering. Nobody cares what your life has gone through. Simply, nobody gives a damn. Okay? You are on your own, fighting in this life alone. You have to win. You must never surrender. If you give in to the hardships in life, you will forever be a failure.

Nobody cares how tough your life may have been. People are busy with their own problems, and they don't have time for you. That you can be sure of. You have to take care of yourself and mind your own business. Stop expecting others to take care of it for you because it will never happen. It's just not the way it's supposed to be. This is the real world where people have to run and run fast every single day just to keep up with the rapid changes. Those who are slow will be left behind. Those who believe in entitlement will be doomed to fail in life because success is not given; it must be earned. Those who care about what others think or say about them are forever distracted by those pointless things.

High Achiever

This world is a cruel place for people who do not have strong discipline and a tough mind. You ought to know better because everybody is fighting for his or her own life. So should you! You have to become the high achiever and the best in the field. You can't afford to be soft and allow yourself to be stripped off your destiny. You are destined to rule, so you must chase your destiny.

Stop feeling sorry for yourself and start working toward your dream. That's all you need to care about. Stop caring whether people care about you or not. They don't, and that's okay. You don't need their pity, whatsoever! You need yourself! You need to work hard for your future. That's all you ever need!

It's okay to change your behaviors or actions if you know what you're doing. People around you don't matter much in your work, so you should not concern yourself with manner issue. It's the least of your concern at work, if you want to know the truth. Having said that, it doesn't mean you should be rude to others either.

The high achievers couldn't care less about what you think of them. They don't give a damn about that! Usually it is the low achievers who care too much about the opinions of others. If you concern yourself too much about too many things that others are saying about you, you won't have time to focus on your work and life. You know that better than anyone else, yet you still forget that part.

Nobody cares about your life and your work. Nobody knows what you're up to, so you don't need to explain everything to everyone. Keep it to yourself and work in silence until you complete your work.

Stay Strong

Get yourself together and be tough. Stay strong and be optimistic! You can do it. You will do it. Don't worry about the current setbacks, for they are only temporary. Don't worry about people's words, for those words won't matter much in your life and your future. Don't worry about anything that has nothing to do with you and your work. You have a life to live and a business to run. You can't be soft. You can't be weak. You have to be tough. You have to be the best in whatever you do. You are the boss of your life, so act like one!

Don't let anyone tell you what to do or how to live your life. You are the boss, and you make the call. You're fully responsible for your life and your work. Stop waiting for approval from anybody else. Stick to what works best for you, and ignore the noises around you. Those noises are everywhere, and everyone can produce so many of them, but you have to block them from getting into your head.

You don't have to be afraid. You just have to do what you want to do now before it's too late. Now it's a good time to start.

Chapter 24
Change
Reverse

I know how you feel about yourself on most days. You feel like a loser because you compare yourself with other people. Especially those who are closer to you. They can be your friends. Your classmates. Your relatives. Or your colleagues. You feel bad because of the fact that you are not as successful as they are, you believe. But you have forgotten who you are and why you are here. You come here for a unique purpose. It's a purpose shared by none, and understood by few even though many people will ridicule you for such a strange idea of life. You have chosen this path, so you shouldn't complain about it, whatsoever.

The best is yet to come, but you have to have faith in yourself and God. You have a different life to live, so you don't have to care if others can see it the same way you do. The fact is, they don't know and they don't care. Period! Why do you care if they agree with you or not? What's the point of that?

You don't need it, and you can't keep worrying about other people's opinions of you. You might be unsure of what to do or how to keep your mind calm while dealing with constant ideas coming from many people around you. Your parents always have some ideas about how you should live your life or what kind of job you should take. They want you to have a good job so that you won't have to be struggling with the same things that they have been dealing with. They want you to find a good partner in marriage and have a good family. In many cases, they are not wrong. They want the best for their child, which is reasonably good. However, if it's not aligned with your value and what you think is best for you, probably it's not a good idea. But how to know whether it's good or not? In other words, one can never know if his or her value is timelessly correct. You have to test it for yourself and see if you're right or not.

Game Changer

One of your ideas might be a game changer, so you have to take these ideas seriously. Pay attention to the result of each one, but don't get married to any of them. Nonetheless, don't get divorced totally from those that have failed to produce the result in the initial stage. They can be reformed and altered in a big way to produce better results. They can be made better and more effective, so to speak.

If you have a better idea of how to do your job, you can try but once again, don't get married to the new idea before it has been proven effective through the test of time. You can test it again and again to see if it really works or it may fall apart in the process. Most ideas which are untested cannot survive the test of time, just so you know.

Thus, it is too soon to say that you should pick up an idea before you test it and fix the errors that occur in the process. Some ideas seem promising at first, but they fall short after a few times of testing. Some don't appear favorable in the beginning, but they have outperformed those that are more appealing.

Don't be afraid to take your chance. You never know when you will get your big break. It is possible that you can be ten times more successful than you ever were. Keep doing your job until you are certain that you have completed your tasks.

Hard times won't last, but you will. As long as you keep going, you will get to where you want to be. As long as you keep going, you will succeed eventually. Don't worry; do the things that you're supposed to do now. Eventually, you'll get the rewards that you're seeking. Do not be discouraged by temporary setbacks. Do not be afraid to retry. You never know; one of those repeated actions can be a game changer.

The irony of life is this: "When you work hard, your life gets easier. If you take it easy, your life will get harder than it should be."

You don't do something because you think you can do it well. You do it because you believe you can do it and you want to prove to yourself. You will see the results of your hard work. You will see them in no time.

However, many things will distract you from your work. Don't let that happen to you. Don't allow anything to ruin your plan for the future. Not to mention people! Especially those with so much drama.

Your Will

You go through life not without big tests to challenge your will. The choice is yours to make, in each step you take. What will you do when you are faced with the toughest decisions in life? Will you cave in or will you be ready for it? Sometimes you are allowed to do things that you want before the things that you have to do. Once in a while you are permitted to do just that. Every now and then, things do not go according to your plan and it couldn't be more painful than to deal with the mess created in the process. What you do is only a part of who you are. What you think is only a part of yourself also. Give yourself enough time to handle your work in a way that is humanly possible. You are not God, but your expectations supersede the way a human being would expect. That's when disappointment comes in to play.

Timeline

You may have a different timeline from most people you know, and that's okay. You make a living doing something that very few people do, so you can't complain about that. Through this job, you have become more disciplined and willfully courageous. But on the surface, there is nothing courageous about your job. It seems like a big mistake, at times.

When the time comes, you will see the purpose of your training. Just keep doing it. Don't quit too soon. In short, don't quit! The money will come in when you open your mind to accept it. So far you haven't done that, and as a result, you have been on the losing side. Maybe something is not right.

Maybe you should fix something now before you can see your next big success. Maybe you are not in alignment with your work and success. Something is wrong; and a thorough change has to be made, and it has to be made as swiftly as possible. You have been on both sides, and you know by instinct what to do.

It's hard to recover the long-lost passion, so don't be afraid to retake the same course of actions that you believe would work for you rather than against you. You can't afford to be soft or to go easy on yourself. Especially when you're supposed to complete the project. Every day, in many ways, you are walking toward the path of no turning back. There is only one path to go and that is to go forward. Choose your next step carefully and be slow to redirect the course, shall anything happen along the way. In each step you take, a sacrifice has to be made. In anything you do, a serious action is needed. In any length of time, a careful calculation has to be in place.

Your Freedom

As a young man, everything was good as long as I could do what I wanted to do. Time, to me, was more important than money. Time equaled freedom to choose. I conserved it as much as possible so that I could use it for something of high value. Or so I thought! I have earned my points, enough to get by at a stable pace. Now everything I do is only the stepping stone for the next project, and I care more about my time because it equals freedom to choose.

If you live your life as if nobody cared about it, you would probably live with complete freedom. You may have a good family, but that will change when you grow up and find new things to add into the priority list. Your parents may have different priorities, however. The other family members may have other matters which do not have anything to do with you at all.

Not to mention society so complex you can't seem to grasp the whole concept. To protect the priorities from eroding, you should be selective with what you see and hear. However, it's a challenging time since the environment around us is more invasive than ever before. If you're lucky, you can avoid many unwanted things that are being constantly fed, but not many people are mindful about receiving such a harmful and toxic waste.

Chapter 25
Money
Money

Many people are quick to complain about their problems in money. They consider themselves poor and want to use poverty as an excuse to rely on the mercy and charity of others. They're not poor, and they don't need help from anyone else. They're just not aware of their own power to control their fate and overcome poverty. Everybody can get out of poverty if he or she wants to! When you have no money, you have nothing to lose. You're free to work and earn money. It might take some time, but you'll make it. You're not poor; keep that in mind. You might be broke for the time being, but that's okay. You might be broke and in debts, but you're not poor. You can use your brain and your muscle to work. Just make sure you won't waste your hard-earned money on useless things like you used to!

Don't take free money from anybody! Just don't! You're not a freeloader, so don't do that. You might be thinking to yourself: "But there's nothing wrong with free money. If somebody is generous enough to give a hundred dollars to me, I'll take the money."

First of all, nobody is dumb enough to do so unless there is a hidden agenda behind that. Second, if you haven't done anything to deserve it, should you take it? Your choice! Do you want to owe others for the rest of your life? Your choice! The money given for nothing is the money owed forever!

NOBODY CARES

Last but not least, you're not poor, and you don't need unnecessary charity or help in that form. And you know that!

When you were a kid, it's an exceptional case because you didn't know any better about the money. Now, as a grown-up person, you know the world better, but most importantly, you know your life better. You want to be free, so you should not let yourself be in debt of the free money from anybody. At first, it doesn't seem like a debt at all, but deep down, you're aware of it. Consciously, you'll be in debt of the person who has given you the money for nothing.

The Rules

If you don't want to be poor, don't take free money from anybody! That's rule number one!

Rule number two: If you don't want to be poor, work hard! It's as simple as that.

Rule number three: If you don't want to be poor, don't spend more than you've earned.

Rule number four: Invest! Invest! Invest! And invest again!

I'm not preaching to anyone on how to be rich, but I'm only offering some ideas about how not to be poor because I hate poverty. In all my life, I've seen enough suffering from people who consider themselves poor and live their lives according to that self-labeling image, which is untrue yet unfair to themselves.

You might have a job but still struggle to pay the bills because it's barely enough money to survive from day to day. But that's not poverty! That's difficulty in money! In other words, you're not poor, but you're just broke. And it's only for the time being.

If you keep working and saving some for the future investment, chances are, you will be able to get out of this temporary financial difficulty.

What I've learned about money is that you are convinced that you're not good enough when you can't earn enough money. The truth is, you're not good enough with money if you spend more than you've earned. It's not the matter of how much you can make, but how much you can keep.

NOBODY CARES

That begs the question: When can you spend what you've saved?

Don't worry about that part because you'll always have things to spend on in the future. Personally, I like to invest in some projects that can pay me back in the future. In the past, I only wanted to make a lot of money. It's a common goal, right? That's true. Now, my only goal is to save a lot of money for the future investment. It's almost similar to the former idea, except for the fact that I can keep the money that I've earned. Very often you can make a lot of money, only to spend it all as soon as you can, and that's why you become broke so often too. But being broke is a good lesson, although you have to learn it the hard way sometimes. Without personal experiences in the lack of money, one can never truly appreciate the importance of saving and investing it.

In conclusion, you should work hard, make more money, save more than you spend, and grow it through good investment.

Chapter 26
Time to Choose
Morning Motivation

The only way for you to reach your greatness in your life is to do what you love and do it every single day, no matter what happens. It's up to you to decide what kind of life you want to have and what kind of goal you want to achieve. It can be hard to do, but it's the way of the world that we live in today. Those who have experienced hardening life will be hardened by it and they shall thrive even when the rest of the world is falling apart.

You can always change and become better when you see the reason you must change. Invest your time till you can reach a new level of your life. Learn a new set of skill, and be different from who you used to be. Spend some time alone if you must, but don't give in to the obstacle of isolation in the darkness. Darkness will try to rule over your life, but you must resist and be in full control. Make a choice to be the champion, not a loser who can't do anything about his life.

Go all in with what you've got and fight this battle, even when you have to fight alone. You're here alone and will remain that way for a long time. You can't run away from it because your life is predestined to be solo. The life that you have chosen is your responsibility; it is your pride also. If you want to make a real difference in your life, you have to be honest with yourself about this solo journey.

You may pretend that your friends are with you because they have shared the same or similar life experiences. Nothing

NOBODY CARES

could be further from the truth. They don't live your life even if they're very close to you. They may be close for now, but you can't expect to be with them forever.

The point is, there will be times when you are alone and must fight for your future alone. No one will help you, but you don't need any help, by the way, so you're doing just fine. Embrace your life as an independent life, and that's the right path to pursue. Don't be trapped by the idea that you can always ask for help from people around you because you can't. Even if you can ask them, it won't guarantee that people will or can help you. if you want to make it to the top, rely on yourself and know that you are in this journey alone.

Don't be afraid to go all in. See what you have to see. Find what you need. Build what you have to build. Create what you don't have. You have the power over your destiny, even in the face of darkness or isolation. You're in it to win it. You have sacrificed enough, and now it's time to get the reward. What are you waiting for? Go all in, and take what you deserve.

Time to Choose

In this life, you have two options to choose: To be successful or to fail forever! But don't get me wrong. Failures can and will get to you every now and then, but among them comes a big success which can make it up to you after all these failing times. However, you can't choose to remain a failure all the time. You shouldn't! The decision is yours to make, so be wise about the direction of your life.

Challenge yourself till you get to the highest level of your life. You can and you should do it. No need to wait for a miracle to happen to you. You don't even need to wait for a good time to get ready. You're ready now, and you can do it now.

Sometimes you don't need to plan it when you're working on something exciting and new. It might be your next big break! It can be a game-changing solution. All you need to do is work on it now. No need to plan for it. Just do the best you can until you get it done. You will find what you are looking for, if you keep doing it. You will see an untapped opportunity, which has been there since day one. It just sits there, waiting for your recognition, by the way! Your job is to connect the dots, so do your job and make your dream come true.

It is possible to get a big reward now because you've worked hard to earn it. Go forward and get your reward. You've earned it! The time is now! Your chance is now! No need to wait any longer! You've waited long enough, by the way. It is possible to get what you deserve, but only if you decide to take it. Now what's your decision?

NOBODY CARES

You'll know what it is when you see it. When you get close, you'll feel it in your mind. Trust your gut instinct! It's always been correct, especially about your success. It calculates the eventual outcome for you, so you can be reassured of your success. Don't worry; do your job, and you'll be successful eventually.

Chapter 27
Time to Create
You Are the Creator

Whatever you lack, create it by yourself because you are the creator. Don't be discouraged by the fact that you have to take more time to get what others might have gotten with little effort. They get it easily because they never have to create it by themselves. You're not a taker, so you can't take something for free. You make it by yourself even if it may take longer time than taking it from someone else.

Hard Times

When you lose hope in yourself, just remember that things are supposed to be hard, not easy. You don't want to remain childish, by the way. Easy life is reserved for childish people only!

Get this: Hard times will make you stronger and tougher! You can't afford to be soft in this world, or, metaphorically speaking, you'll be ripped apart by everything that comes to get you. Believe me, there is always something that wants a piece of you. If you're not tough enough, you'll be eaten alive by it. There is nothing you can do to stop it if you're soft. Be strong and be tough in whatever that you're doing, and never surrender to anything.

Hopelessness

Even in the face of hopelessness, you should never surrender your will to it. You are strong enough to fight back. And fight back, you must! The real power is from within you, and only you can wield it. But only when your free will is still yours to command can you use this power to your advantage. The glory of success is yours to make, but only when you know the right path to take. There comes a time when you are lost and unsure of what to do next, but don't worry because you shall get through it. It's only for the time being.

You have a job to do, and that is to fight for your life and your future. Don't let anything stop you from reaching your full potential in this life. Don't even allow your weak self to convince you otherwise.

At times it feels like a dream, but only the one that remains stuck in your mind and hasn't come true yet. You have to do something about it, or it will forever be a dream. Don't fall into the idea that you can wait till it comes to you because it won't. No great dream can come to you without your acknowledgment. Let alone your acceptance! Don't make the same mistake that many people have done. Don't ignore your dream.

Keep Moving

The way to get to the finished line is to keep moving until you get there. It's that simple. More often than not, you might feel like it is an uphill battle because it is. You have to fight hard, and you have to fight with your heart. You have to use everything you've got if you want to win this war.

When you fall down, get up. When you fall down again, get up one more time. Never ever quit on yourself! For better or for worse, experiences will shape your way of thinking. Do something that you're inspired to do even when it's difficult in the beginning. Not to mention in the process! You can never predict what will come out of it.

Along the way, there will be many obstacles standing in your way, but you can't allow them to stop you from doing what you want to do in your life, no matter how hard it may seem. The best is yet to come, and you'd better be ready when it does.

Don't let anyone tell you what to do because no one knows more about you than you do. Choose your own path, and walk toward it.

There will be days when you lose faith. Days when you have no idea what your life is going to be. But those days won't deter you from doing what you're sent to do on this Earth. You either stick to it, or you will be stuck with something else that you do not want. If you don't want to get driven far from your goal, you should ignore things that are not helping you get there. Instead, you must focus on your goal, and nothing else.

Ignore Your Pain

Ignore your pain too, when you must, but do not think, even for once, that you can live free from it. Pain is a part of your job. It takes great pain to get the job done, and you know that. Do your job, and don't worry about anything else, for you should get there when the time is right. You just keep doing your job every day now. Okay?

Work on your skills every single day. Never be satisfied with your current results, for they can be replaced any time by someone else's work that is better. You have to outwork everyone and remain at the top forever. You can't afford to be complacent, regardless of how great you are. You'll never know. Someday a new kid in the block may try to steal the glory from you by outworking and outsmarting you. You can't allow that to happen! Work hard, and stay at the top! To be successful, a lot of sacrifice has to be made, but it is only for the time being. You can afford it, by the way. But you can't be successful in one thing when your brain is busy dealing with many things that are, at best irrelevant and, at worst, useless. A lot of people have done that because they fail to see the importance of focus. Focus is the key to success, but focus is impossible if your mind is distracted by many things at the same time.

Chapter 28
Maturity Transformation

When you are younger than 20 years old, all you care about is education. It's your priority, but it's only a preparation for another stage of life. When you are younger than 25 years old and have your first job, you should be proud of yourself because you are transitioning into maturity and fully responsible for your life and choices. When you are younger than 30 years old and you have a stable relationship, you should be blessed because you are stable and certain of your future.

When you are mature enough, you don't get upset over small matters with your parents like you were back in the old days as you were younger and immature.

It's okay if your parents are not fully supportive of your plans or even actions. When you have successfully achieved your goals, you don't have to remind them that you were right then and you are right now. They'll surely know even if they wouldn't admit it.

Don't take it too personally when your mom doesn't believe in what you believe. You know better than she does, but you don't have to explain everything to her. Wait till you have completed it, and let your results speak for themselves.

When everyone else is questioning your ability to do things, you must not listen to them. You have your own ideas, and you can prove them wrong.

How many friends do you have and can trust? Few? How much do you value in friendship? Not much? Is it even important to have friends?

If you were a lonely person in your childhood times, you might know how to deal with loneliness when you're at the top and successful. Family and friendship are two different elements in life, by the way.

Between the age of 22 to 29 years old, I never thought that going outside to meet people was that important. I work from home, so I never had to go out unless I had an important appointment, which I rarely had. I mean, if people wanted to see me, they had to come to my home and talk to me. That's me. When I'm turning 30 years old, surprisingly, my idea about this issue has changed dramatically. I have no problem going out every single day now. I go to the gym, for example. I go out and buy something to eat.

It's better to stick to what you know best than to allow your attention to scatter randomly through many opportunities being thrown at you. In other words, you should become the expert of your trade rather than to trade your skills for chump change. However, to become the expert in what you do is not without a price. In fact, it comes with a big and non-negotiable price, and that price is hard work.

When dealing with your tasks, it's wise to prioritize, regardless of the importance alone. It has to be both important and timely. Otherwise, you'll face an avoidable failure. Control your time through the tasks that you choose to do at a particular moment. In the past, most of your failures came from the mishandling of the tasks, leaving you little time and energy to complete the right ones in a timely manner.

NOBODY CARES

Regardless of your creativeness, you'll never overcome this problem if you do not prioritize your tasks. On top of that, you should arrange them according to the nature of the necessity rather than feelings. Many people have done things in accordance with their feelings, and they end up being overwhelmed by those unfinished tasks while the deadlines were approaching closer. As a result to that, they had to abandon some of those tasks in the hope that they could summon all their strength and conserve as much time as they could to finish the few remaining tasks. It happened a lot, and it had become the habit. These people become the victims of their feelings and emotions.

To reverse that, you need to be careful about how you spend your time. Learn to calculate every small detail that you do each day. At first, it feels dumb to do so, but soon enough, you'll learn the hidden effect that will help you in the end.

One more thing, you should study the patterns of your thoughts and actions because they serve the same purpose: Growth!

However, sometimes instead of enhancing your life, some of your actions are detrimental to the development of growth. Pay attention to those actions, and change them when you can. Some are hard to change, and some are only the products of temporary turbulence. But all of them are changeable when you really want to change them. Use your willpower. Change one thing at a time. Don't rush. But don't quit.

Sometimes a small change can make a big difference in your life, but it has to be purely from your heart that you want to change it. Otherwise, it will be a vain attempt.

Start from something small or easy first, and go on to fix the big and stubborn ones. You'll get there as you try harder. No problem is too big to deal with. No mountain is too high to climb. No challenge is too insurmountable to overcome. But you must use your willpower to deal with these problems.

Once again, manage your time and control your tasks so that you can have more successes and fewer failures along the way. Arrange your time and tasks accordingly.

One more thing, I have noticed some changes in my habits of work and socializing. The truth is, I don't socialize that much. By that, I mean, not at all. If it wasn't for work, I wouldn't have invested my time to talk or text with people online. I just don't have the time or interest in it. It's boring and it's distracting to me.

I'd rather spend all the time I have to write or read something from books. It's how I live my life and I intend to keep it that way. I don't mind a lonely lifestyle as long as I can work with what I love to do. I don't like distraction, and I hate annoyance. This is why I spend a good amount of time trying to avoid all of those things that distract me or slow me down from my work. But it's not always easy to avoid such things, especially in a connected world like this one. It makes you feel guilty for not responding to people's messages even when you don't have the time or attention to do so. But each of us has this sense of obligation to respond to other people, and soon enough we have developed this habit of connecting with them digitally. Sometimes it's good, but most of the time, it's bad because it's so overwhelming that you could barely breathe and have time for yourself or your work. It's true that people are,

NOBODY CARES

in some ways, forcing one another to get connected and be distracted by things that are not always good or benefiting.

Those who are smart enough not to get deeply connected with online world are the few people who can manage their lives and times better. I'm not saying that they can't go online for a while. Of course, they can and they do. But the level of engagement with digital world is much less than other people. In other words, they don't care much about the digital world.

Chapter 29
Because I Am Weird
My Experience with Digital World

My experiences with digital world and social media are not always explainable to most people since they have been engaging with online world long enough. They can't stay away from it longer than an hour, except for when they're sleeping or their phones or computers are dead. The world we live in today is a world full of information, good and bad in combination. Nobody can fully escape from it, but of course, we can manage our urge. Even though it's not easy to control the impulse to use social media, you can try decreasing it.

Information is like food. What you get from social media is like street food. You don't know if that information is good or garbage, but you cannot tell the differences if the channels or sites from which you get the information are somehow good at photoshopping or editing. That's the harsh reality of today's world. The most annoying of all is the information that you see from random posts when you're scrolling down. It happens, a lot.

I don't scroll down my Facebook newsfeed, by the way. I mean, rarely do I have interest in scrolling it. However, I do see a few things on newsfeed, but it is automatic display because when you get into the app, you'll be directed into the newsfeed before anything else. It appears in front of your eyes automatically, regardless of your interest.

NOBODY CARES

However, I cannot say the same thing about Instagram because I actually scroll down the newsfeed from this app. The reason is obvious; I'm lazy to type the names of the very few pages of the regular news pages which I read the stories from. But that's it. Nothing else! Besides, I get annoyed by the advertisements that appear every three posts that I scroll down. Three or four, I'm not sure. But they are there by default.

The point is, when you scroll down the newsfeed, you get distracted by things that are not in your agenda. That's when you're wasting your time. I don't like wasting my time, so I don't like scrolling through newsfeed, on social media.

Maybe I'm a bad social media user, I guess. That's why I don't spend much of my time on it. I mean, I get bored too fast and too easily. Sometimes I even try to get interested in it, but I can't. I just can't spend longer than an hour on it. I'm talking about scrolling through the newsfeed.

You might be wondering what am I doing on Facebook, right? Well, I post some statuses, check my notifications, and messenger chat. These are the reasons why I spend less time on social media, and easily get bored. Sometimes I do want to connect there longer, but it's just impossible for me because my habits on social media has been this way for too long.

You would ask: "*How can you connect with your friends, Mr. Author?*"

Well, I call them or usually meet in person. I can spend more than three hours talking to my friends in person, but I can't text or chat with them longer than 5 minutes. That's the reality of my friendship, and they understand that perfectly well. But the truth is, I can type on my phone or computer so fast that I can save me plenty of time to text than to talk in person, but I still prefer real talk with real person. It's a force of habit, I suppose!

One more thing, I'm good at ignoring people's messages. I can leave those messages unread for days before I check and reply them. The reason is obvious: I forget that social media still exist.

It sounds dumb, but it is true.

I don't know why people are so addicted to social media. Like, for real. But I don't bother to ask anyone because it's none of my business.

My habit of learning about someone on social media usually makes it a distinctive difference from the rest of the users because instead of scrolling random posts about random people, I go straight to the timeline of one user and learn about that person from what he or she has posted or shared. Sometimes I just check on my old friends and see what they've been doing, but I rarely leave a comment or anything on their posts. They don't know that I know! But that's okay because they don't care! Neither do I!

Chapter 30
Nobody Cares Nobody Cares

Work hard every waking hour. Work harder than you have ever done before. You have a long way to go, and your success is built through repetition of hard work. Don't let anyone talk you out of this. You have to fight and fight hard for your future. You have to power to alter your life condition from bad to good. But first, you have to decide to follow that path. Do not rely on chance.

It's okay to stay away from the world for a while. It's okay to focus on your work until you're ready to show it to the world. There is nothing wrong with that.

Your mind limits your life. But the same mind that limits your life possibilities can be the tool to broaden your life too. That begs the question: "How to use your mind to work for you rather than against you?"

Nobody cares if you have a big problem or just peanuts, but you have to work and provide what you promise.

Nobody cares if you have to deal with mountains of issues being placed on your shoulders. People expect results from you. That's non-negotiable!

Nobody cares if you're rich or in debt, but you have to pay what you owe.

Nobody cares if you're sick or temporarily unwell physically or mentally, but you have to do what you have promised you would do.

Nobody cares if you're feeling down or stressed out. You've got to do what you've got to do in order to complete your goal. It's you against you right now. You must win over your soft side and rule your life.

Nobody cares if you're in pain or not. You have to be strong. You have to get up and fight harder. You have to fight for your life. And you have to fight for your future.

Nobody cares if you're angry or not, but you have to keep calm and deal with life problems with a fair mind. Not a clouded mind, by the way! Swallow your pride and be cool and calm. You have the right to be angry but nobody will care. Period!

Nobody cares about your little misery; you have to deal with it. You can't rely on anyone, and you know that.

Nobody cares if you're right or wrong, but you have to make your point and prove that you're right. Keep working on your work until you make a breakthrough.

Nobody cares if you're upset or not; you have to keep it to yourself.

Nobody cares if you're happy or sad. People are busy with their own problems and don't have time or attention for you or anyone else, for that matter. What gives you the idea that you can take away their time for your own problems? What makes you think you can steal someone else's time? You wouldn't want anyone else to do the same to you, would you? Get realistic, and respect someone else's time.

Nobody cares if you're very good at what you do if you do not provide value to people in need of your products.

Suggestion from Machine

Nobody cares if you have a big problem right now. People are busy with their own problems. That's the truth!

Suggestion from Machine: "Deal with your problem by yourself. You're strong enough to do so."

Be strong!

Be optimistic!

Be thoughtful!

Be true!

You might be wondering: "How can I be strong in the face of so many problems?"

I get it, you're dealing with many things unpleasant at this point. It's a tough time, but it shall pass. However, it'll only leave you alone if you have a strong willpower and refuse to give in to those problems.

You might not have the power to choose [or stop] the kinds of problems that would come into your life, but clearly, you have the power to choose the ways to deal with those problems.

A strong will is your strength, so choose to be strong and be willing to fight back against those problems. If God is with you, who else can break your spirit? Nobody!

Because I am too busy!

Don't miss out!

Visit the website below and you can sign up to receive emails whenever Dara Ly publishes a new book. There's no charge and no obligation.

https://books2read.com/r/B-A-HAXZ-QEURC

BOOKS2READ

Connecting independent readers to independent writers.

About the Publisher

Milton Keynes UK
Ingram Content Group UK Ltd.
UKHW040215160324
439374UK00004B/255